C A P S T O N E

 W9-CTU-740

Stay Smart!

Smart things to know about... is a complete library of the world's smartest business ideas. **Smart** books put you on the inside track to the knowledge and skills that make the most successful people tick.

Each book brings you right up to speed on a crucial business issue.
The subjects that business people tell us they most want to master are:

Smart Things to Know About **Brands and Branding**	JOHN MARIOTTI
Smart Things to Know About **Business**	JAMES LEIBERT
Smart Things to Know About **Business Finance**	KEN LANGDON
Smart Things to Know About **Change**	DAVID FIRTH
Smart Things to Know About **Consultancy**	PATRICK FORSYTH
Smart Things to Know About **CRM**	DAVID HARVEY
Smart Things to Know About **Culture**	DONNA DEEPROSE
Smart Things to Know About **Customers**	ROS JAY
Smart Things to Know About **Decision Making**	KEN LANGDON
Smart Things to Know About **E-Business**	MIKE CUNNINGHAM
Smart Things to Know About **E-commerce**	MIKE CUNNINGHAM
Smart Things to Know About **Growth**	TONY GRUNDY
Smart Things to Know About **Innovation and Creativity**	DENNIS SHERWOOD
Smart Things to Know About **Knowledge Management**	THOMAS KOULOPOULOS
Smart Things to Know About **Leadership**	JONATHAN YUDELOWITZ
Smart Things to Know About **Life Long-learning**	ANDREW HOLMES
Smart Things to Know About **Managing Projects**	DONNA DEEPROSE
Smart Things to Know About **Marketing**	JOHN MARIOTTI
Smart Things to Know About **Mergers & Acquisitions**	TONY GRUNDY
Smart Things to Know About **Motivation**	DONNA DEEPROSE
Smart Things to Know About **Partnerships**	JOHN MARIOTTI
Smart Things to Know About **People Management**	DAVID FIRTH
Smart Things to Know About **Scenario Planning**	TONY KIPPENBERGER
Smart Things to Know About **Six Sigma**	ANDREW BERGER
Smart Things to Know About **Strategy**	RICHARD KOCH
Smart Things to Know About **Managing Talent**	STEPHANIE OVERMAN
Smart Things to Know About **Teams**	ANNEMARIE CARRACIOLO
Smart Things to Know About **Technology Management**	ANDREW HOLMES
Smart Things to Know About **Your Career**	JOHN MIDDLETON

You can stay **Smart** by e-mailing us at **info@wiley-capstone.co.uk**
Let us keep you up to date with new Smart books, Smart updates, a Smart newsletter
and Smart seminars and conferences. Get in touch to discuss your needs.

CAPSTONE

·INSTANT·
KNOWLEDGE

Smart
THINGS TO KNOW ABOUT ·➔

Life-long
Learning

ANDREW HOLMES

Copyright © Andrew Holmes 2003

The right of Andrew Holmes to be identified as the author of this book has been asserted in accordance with the Copyright, Designs and Patents Act 1988

First Published 2003 by
Capstone Publishing Limited (a Wiley company)
8 Newtec Place
Magdalen Road
Oxford
OX4 1RE
United Kingdom
http://www.capstoneideas.com

All Rights Reserved. Except for the quotation of small passages for the purposes of criticism and review, no part of this publication may be reproduced, stored in a retrieval system or transmitted in any form or by any means, electronic, mechanical, photocopying, recording, scanning or otherwise, except under the terms of the Copyright, Designs and Patents Act 1988 or under the terms of a licence issued by the Copyright Licensing Agency Ltd, 90 Tottenham Court Road, London W1T 4LP, UK, without the permission in writing of the Publisher. Requests to the Publisher should be addressed to the Permissions Department, John Wiley & Sons Ltd, The Atrium, Southern Gate, Chichester, West Sussex, PO19 8SQ, England, or emailed to permreq@wiley.co.uk, or faxed to (+44) 1243 770571.

CIP catalogue records for this book are available from the British Library and the US Library of Congress

ISBN 1-84112-425-7

Typeset in 11/15pt Sabon by Sparks Computer Solutions Ltd, Oxford, UK (http://www.sparks.co.uk)
Printed and bound by T.J. International Ltd, Padstow, Cornwall

Substantial discounts on bulk quantities of Capstone Books are available to corporations, professional associations and other organizations. For details telephone Capstone Publishing on (+44-1865-798623), fax (+44-1865-240941) or email (info@wiley-capstone.co.uk).

Contents

What is Smart?

The *Smart* series is a new way of learning. *Smart* books will improve your understanding and performance in some of the critical areas you face today like *customers, strategy, change, e-commerce, brands, influencing skills, knowledge management, finance, teamworking,* and *partnerships*.

Smart books summarize accumulated wisdom as well as providing original cutting-edge ideas and tools that will take you out of theory and into action.

The widely respected business guru Chris Argyris points out that even the most intelligent individuals can become ineffective in organizations. Why? Because we are so busy working that we fail to learn about ourselves. We stop reflecting on the changes around us. We get sucked into the patterns of behaviour that have produced success for us in the past, not realizing that it may no longer be appropriate for us in the fast-approaching future.

There are three ways the *Smart* series helps prevent this happening to you:

- by increasing your self awareness;

- by developing your understanding, attitude and behaviour; and

- by giving you the tools to challenge the status quo that exists in your organization.

Smart people need smart organizations. You could spend a third of your career hopping around in search of the Holy Grail, or you could begin to create your own smart organization around you today.

Finally, a reminder that books don't change the world, people do. And although the *Smart* series offers you the brightest wisdom from the best practitioners and thinkers, these books throw the responsibility on you to *apply* what you're learning to your work.

Because the truly smart person knows that reading a book is the start of the process and not the end ...

As Eric Hoffer says, 'In times of change, learners inherit the world, while the learned remain beautifully equipped to deal with a world that no longer exists.'

David Firth
Smartmaster

Introduction –
It's Time to Wise Up

For literally millennia, our very survival depended upon our ability to work the land. Physical toil was the mainstay of the population. During this time, power resided in those that owned the land, rather than in those that toiled upon it. And it was only in the aftermath of the Black Death in the fourteenth century, which killed at least a third of Europe's population, that landlords found the balance of power had shifted to those serfs still alive and capable of work. However, despite the concessions that followed, the shift of power from landlord to serf was short-lived.

The truly momentous changes occurred with the agricultural revolution of the eighteenth century and the Industrial Revolution of the nineteenth century, which shifted power from the landowners to the financiers. The process of transforming the workforce into what we have today also started: although at this time the majority of people still worked the land, an increasing number worked in factories, with machinery that needed tending and maintenance. Not only did this require specialist skills, it also necessitated changes in the nature of work, especially in relation to how workers updated their skills in order to remain in employment. As to be expected in times of great change, those without the requisite skills or adaptability found themselves out of work. In some cases, the displaced workers reacted violently as with the anti-factory Luddite movement in England. Such extreme reaction was generated by the feeling of hopelessness that was caused by the rapidity of change and the limited skills that the average worker possessed at that time. It should also be remembered that power resided in the factory owners and their financial backers, rather than in those that sweated in the factories.

All of this changed with the emergence of the computer during the 1950s. It was this that unleashed the current shift in work patterns, the heralding of the information age and the increasing dependence on knowledge and a knowledgeable workforce. United States Census Bureau data illustrates this very well. Between 1900 and 1980, the percentage of farm workers fell from 37.5 per cent in 1900 to 2.8 per cent in 1980. Over the same period, the percentage involved with manual and service work remained pretty static, barely moving at all (44.9 to 45.0 per cent). But white-collar work grew from 17.6 to 52.2 per cent over these 80 years.[1] These days, our well-being depends less on what we can do, and more on what we know. Harnessing our intellectual capital is now the most important skill in an ever-complex workplace.

The process of change accelerated dramatically during the last decades of the twentieth century. The increasingly wired world that stimulated the globalization of commerce brought with it new challenges for governments, organizations and especially individuals. No longer sheltered from the vagaries of economic downturn overseas, each has been subject to the rapid and brutal swings of the global economy. For many people this has resulted in them being downsized (or 'right-sized' as it is termed today) as major corporations cut headcount in order to improve profitability and competitiveness. For those that remain in employment, their working lives have become more insecure, less responsible and, if we are brutally honest with ourselves, less fun. But as well as the coarse changes that have occurred, such as headcount reduction, there are more subtle ones which have arisen from the increasing use of technology, such as the dumbing down of the workforce.

In general we are all pretty good at recognizing and responding to single issues and events. But we tend to be poor at dealing with multiple factors simultaneously and understanding the implications of trends. It is the longer-term, multi-factor changes that reduce the shelf-life of the average employee, especially if they are not paying attention. What has also shifted is the nature of change itself. It has many more facets and is increasingly more complex and difficult to analyze. So although equipped for today, the typical worker is rarely equipped for tomorrow. Especially as they and their employers become locked into the short-term thinking frame of mind that has been created by the rapidly changing financial markets.

The majority of us are unprepared for significant change and, rather than tackle it head on, we tend to allow the changes to pass us by, or we decide to emotionally and psychologically check out of work when it gets too tough.

SMART PEOPLE TO HAVE ON YOUR SIDE:

STEWART BRAND

- Author of *The Clock of the Long Now*, which describes the creation of a clock that measures centuries, not seconds.
- Believes society has developed a dangerously short attention span.
- Sees six significant levels of pace and size in the working structure of a robust and adaptable civilization:
  - fashion (shortest);
  - commerce;
  - infrastructure;
  - governance;
  - culture; and
  - nature (longest).

Clearly there is little merit in either of these strategies because as we as individuals suffer, so do our employers and, ultimately, so does the country in which we live. After all, we are living in an increasingly intensive and unforgiving global economy that gives few second chances.

We all need to wise up to the implications of a rapidly changing workplace. We can no longer leave school or university and think, 'that's the end of my learning; I'm off to the real world of work.' The reality is that we all have to update our skills and knowledge on a continuous basis. Failure to do so could, in extreme cases, leave you on the bap heap (a euphemistic term for having all but limited employment opportunities, usually associated with flipping burgers). Key to wising up and ensuring we have long-term employment prospects is embracing lifelong learning and breaking out from the learning barriers (real or perceived) put in our way by our previous experiences of the education system. Preparing for the changes ahead requires us to become much more adaptable and willing to learn. And, who knows, it might be fun too.

Smart quotes

Learning is the process of individuals constructing and transforming experience into knowledge, skills, attitudes, values, beliefs, emotions …

Peter Jarvis

If we are to embrace lifelong learning we need to understand what learning actually means. This is important because we all tend to lose sight of the importance of learning and allow our learning skills to become rusty. Everyone's learning begins within the family setting. During our early childhood we are influenced heavily by our parents as they encourage the exploration of new ideas within a safe and risk-free environment. At this stage of our development we absorb huge amounts of information and learn geometrically. Our minds are open and accept every new experience at face value. Our formal learning begins when we enter nursery school and continues through primary, secondary, and, for an increasing number of people, tertiary education. The impact of this formal learning process on our attitudes should not be underestimated because it is here that we start to

Q: Why is it so important to learn continuously?

A: The Organisation for Economic Co-operation and Development (OECD) have found that better-educated people are more likely to be in work and less likely to be unemployed than those who are less well-educated.[2]

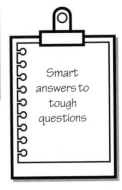

Smart answers to tough questions

develop our prejudices towards learning and education. If these prejudices are strong then we fail to embrace learning once we complete our formal education. The opposite is also true, as if we feel inspired by our experience of learning, we tend to carry our thirst for knowledge into adulthood. And one of the principal purposes of the tertiary education system is to develop our skills in self-directed learning.

Despite the essential foundations that the formal education and learning process provides, learning often takes a back seat once we enter the workplace. And for some it stops altogether, either because learning seems to have lost its importance, or they have been turned off by 10–15 years of hard slog in the classroom. Instead, we become defined by our work and the need to hold down our jobs, pay our bills, bring up children and cope with the rigours of working life. Within the work setting, learning becomes restricted to understanding the bare essentials of a particular process, system, operation, or function. As a result, learning, when it takes place, is narrowly focused. Life becomes routine; a succession of events not much different from the last. As a result, we all get comfortable working for the same employer, executing the same tasks and spending time with the same people. But given the impacts of technological change and globalization (see Chapter 1), this type of existence is increasingly tenuous. Also, as the rate of change increases, our ability to cope with the future reduces because we are unused to learning, unlearning and relearning at an accelerated rate. It is no wonder, then, that workers are more stressed than ever before, feel out of control, and are generally fearful of their future. But at the same time, we hear of skill shortages, graduates who are poorly prepared for the modern workplace, and the need to continuously reinvent ourselves through continuous learning. Clearly, there is a major problem that needs to be addressed.

Therefore, the real challenge for us all is how we go about upgrading and transforming our skills to maintain our employability throughout our careers. People with outdated vocational skills and attitudes will find it increasingly difficult to maintain their levels of income, or, in some cases, any income at all. We are already witnessing the gradual decline in benefits, pay and quality of work for a large proportion of white-collar workers in the United States. And the disparity in income between the rich and poor is increasing at an ever faster rate. For example, United States Census Bureau reports that the disparity is at its highest since World War II. Today, the top 20 per cent of Americans receive half the income of the country, whilst middle-income families have seen their household income drop by four per cent between 1989 and 1996.[3] Only those at the high-end of the knowledge economy seem to be increasing their prospects. These are the consultants, investment bankers and board-level executives. The people most at risk are those who are some 10, 20 or 30 years into their careers who have failed

KILLER QUESTIONS

WHAT ARE YOU GOING TO DO TO MAKE SURE YOU ARE EMPLOYABLE TEN YEARS FROM NOW?

The good news is that it is possible to respond by developing the mental adaptability we had as children and that was honed during our formal education. Learning, unlearning and relearning does not have to be a chore and the economic benefits to the individual can be significant. Lifelong learning is the key to longevity within the workplace and the essential foundation of the learning organization. Those that develop the ability to continuously learn will inherit the organization of the future. In doing so they will be able to adapt more readily to the changing business environment and maintain their upward careers.

to assess their skills in relation to the wider economy and market place. Why is this such a problem? Because most training and retraining is geared toward the young, not the mid-career professional who could benefit the most. It is clear that new jobs demanding old skills will not materialize; new jobs require new skills. With governments and organizations generally slow to respond to these issues, it is up to the individual to ensure they are appropriately skilled throughout their careers. No one else cares, and if they do, it is mainly rhetoric.

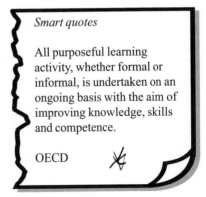

Smart quotes

All purposeful learning activity, whether formal or informal, is undertaken on an ongoing basis with the aim of improving knowledge, skills and competence.

OECD

Understanding what lifelong learning is all about

The term 'lifelong learning' originated approximately ten years ago within the OECD which was seeking to place emphasis on outputs (learning) rather than inputs (education, training and self-study). But before we say what lifelong learning is, it is necessary to say what it isn't. Lifelong learning is not another name for training, nor is it just another management fad.

Training – the process of acquiring the knowledge and skills related to work requirements using formal, structured or guided means, but excluding general supervision, job-specific innovations and learning by experience ... Training lies within the domain of organization: it is an intervention designed to produce behaviours from individuals that have positive organizational results ...

Learning – the physical and mental process involved in changing one's normal behavioural patterns and habits ... Learning lies within the domain of the individual, can result from a whole range of experiences, and can be positive, negative or neutral from the organization's point of view.

Martyn Sloman

Smart quotes

By the same token, lifelong learning is not about continuing professional development (CPD). CPD is an increasingly important aspect of a professional's life and for some, failing to maintain their CPD can result in expulsion from their profession. But the key point about CPD is that it is imposed by the professional institution and as a result, only a small percentage of professionals take up the CPD programmes on offer. According to one review, only 10–20 per cent of professionals ever take part and their number is usually made up of the same people.[4] And, like training, this can be a somewhat passive exercise, with limited learning value. For example, it is possible to class the attendance at a conference as CPD, but one could attend and learn nothing. Keeping a log of such activities merely indicates that you have attended. It does not necessarily mean you have learnt something. Because the profession drives CPD, it is not sufficiently focused on the individual. This raises a very important point about lifelong learning: it is a very personal affair. Learning is an active process, involves choice (that is whether you want to learn or not), and cannot be enforced. It is up to you whether you want to embrace learning, no one else. Thus, things like CPD miss the point because they are imposed upon the professional community.

There is one other issue that serves to confuse the debate on lifelong learning and this is its focus. Policy makers like to state that lifelong learning is focused on learning throughout your whole life, from birth through to death. This is, of course, laudable, but from a personal perspective, its primary focus should be on the learning that is associated with our working lives. Eddy Knasel, John Meed and Anna Rossetti in their book *Learn for Your Life,* help to clear up some of the confusion by making the distinction between career, lifelong and life-wide learning:

- Career learning is often directly associated with work, careers and their management.

- Life-wide/lifetime learning is the term most often used by policy makers to describe the provision of education and training for people throughout their working lives.

- Lifelong learning is learning that occurs throughout a person's life.

For our purposes, I define lifelong learning as both an attitude and a discipline that extends beyond vocational and work-focused on-the-job training, and which encapsulates the softer skills such as interpersonal communication, teamwork, emotional intelligence and problem solving. Lifelong learning is principally focused on maintaining longevity within ones working life, and is controlled by the individual, but influenced by the organization. This definition is more akin to life-wide and lifetime learning, but goes further by placing the responsibility on the individual. Ultimately, for those in work, lifelong learning will always take on a work focus. There is, of course, nothing to stop you learning other things at any stage of your life, but the real thrust of lifelong learning is about future proofing your career.

SMART PEOPLE
TO HAVE ON
YOUR SIDE:

BOB GARRETT

- Learning organization thought leader.
- Author of *The Learning Organization, Learning to Lead* and *The Fish Rots From the Head*.
- He believes there are four preconditions to successful organizational learning:
  1. Everyone in the organization has to be encouraged to learn from their daily work and, more importantly, time is set aside to do so.
  2. Systems and processes must be in place that can capture learning, share it, celebrate it and use it.
  3. The organization as a whole should be encouraged to transform itself through its internal and external learning processes.
  4. Learning should be valued in the appraisal process and included within people's compensation.

The many forms of lifelong learning

Because lifelong learning is an inherently personal affair, there is no single model on which to base your learning. However, we should all recognize that learning can be planned as well as accidental and we should therefore be sufficiently sensitive and open-minded to the learning opportunities around us. Such opportunities fall into the following categories:

- Personal development – the way we as individuals develop our interpersonal and intra-personal skills and capabilities.

- Planned development – following formal courses, such as degrees, MBAs, technical qualifications and so on. This also includes the various forms of training received during our working lives.

- Accidental development – unplanned learning that occurs during the course of our working lives.

- Experience-based development – learning by doing. This would include advancing skills and capabilities through practice as well as learning new ones by observing others who have them and using these people as role models.

Unwrapping this further suggests we can learn from a variety of sources including:

- Customers – often the only way we find out about our products and services is through customers and they are one of the principal drivers behind such things as customer relationship management.

- Colleagues – a great source of insight and one of the few ways to articulate and release much of the tacit knowledge that exists in organizations.

- Success – there is always the danger that success breeds arrogance. But success does provide a golden opportunity to develop an understanding of how and why it came about and to use this to model the process through which it was achieved.

- Failure – although always painful, failure provides the perfect opportunity for learning as long as we have the stomach to do so and are prepared to face up to our flaws and inadequacies.

- Books – obvious to state, and yet only a small minority of people bother to read widely. Most buy books and then allow them to gather dust on their shelves or restrict their reading to just newspapers and fiction. This is not good enough.

- Daily routines – experience is one of the most effective ways of learning anything new, and our daily routine is often a relatively safe environment within which to test new ideas.

- Projects – if you are fortunate to be involved with projects, they are a perfect way to learn about the corporation, innovation and politics. If you are not involved with projects, seek them out, but be warned, working on projects is very different from working in a single functional area. They are stressful, hard work, but ultimately very rewarding.

Q: What's so great about lifelong learning? What will it bring to me and my company?

A: Learning used to be only for those who wanted to progress in the workplace. Gaining additional qualifications, such as MBAs showed a willingness to grow personally and professionally. These were important qualities for those who wanted to be the company's future leaders. Advances in technology, globalization and the uncertainties of the global economy mean that everybody must be willing to continuously update their skills. Here are just some of the benefits …

Smart answers to tough questions

Benefits for the smart individual

- Increased career choices.

- Enhanced employability.

- Real opportunity to increase earnings.

- Increased job satisfaction.

- Enhanced self-awareness and personal growth.

- Long-term survival in an increasingly competitive workplace.

Benefits for the smart organization

- Increased flexibility that comes from a well-educated workforce. This translates into a healthy bottom line. For example, companies that invest in learning typically outperform the market by 45 per cent, whilst companies that don't, underperform it by 22 per cent.

- Higher retention rates, which reduce employment costs. Given that the average cost of losing an employee is $50,000, it would make sense to reduce turnover to a reasonable level, never zero perhaps, but focused on retaining the brightest and best.

- Only 12 per cent of employees plan to leave an employer that offers excellent training opportunities. Compare that to the 41 per cent who plan to leave organizations that offer either low levels of training or training which is considered to be of poor quality.[5]

- More productive staff who are willing to get involved with changing the organization for the better.

- Learning faster and becoming smarter – continuously changing and enhancing what they do.

- Long-term survival in the increasingly competitive global economy.

Being successful at lifelong learning

According to Alastair Rylatt, author of *Learning Unlimited*, a commitment to learning requires a commitment to other things, including:

- a desire to make a difference;

- being open to discovery of new options;

- taking risks;

- being tolerant to the uncertainty of modern times; and

- a commitment to unlearn and forget those things we know that are no longer relevant or which are preventing us from accepting new ideas.

Back in 1995, Bill Gates dismissed the Internet as an irrelevance, and yet a few years later, when the significance of the Internet was clear, he was able to mobilize his entire organization to take on the established players. This required Microsoft to unlearn their entrenched views of what the Internet meant and accept the new world order that it represented. This required them to learn and apply new concepts.

Smart things to think about

This book is probably different from the others you may have read on this subject. In this book I hope to challenge you as well as give you enough information on which to base your own career decisions and self-direct your learning. So, as well as providing you with a clear understanding of why lifelong learning matters, I will also describe how you can develop and implement a lifelong learning strategy. Along the way I will cover many topics. Some of these will relate directly to the learning process, whilst others will not. The purpose of this is to provide you with an enriched perspective of the importance and practicalities of lifelong learning. At the end of the book you should be well armed to cope with, and even influence, the changes before you. I believe that we should all be aiming for a more satisfying, financially rewarding and interesting career. Standing still is not an option. Of course, if you want to career that is defined by uncertainty, job loss, and low interest then put this book down now; it's not for you.

Smart quotes

The greatest difficulty in the world is not for people to accept new ideas, but to make them forget about old ideas.

John Maynard Keynes

Notes

1 Cortada, J. (1998) *Rise of the Knowledge Worker*. Woburn MA: Butterworth-Heinemann, pp. 72–9.

2 OECD (2001) *The Well-being of Nations: The Role of Human and Social Capital*. Paris: OECD, p. 28.

3 Rifkin, J. (2000) *The Age of Access: How the Shift from Ownership to Access is Transforming Modern Life*. London: Penguin Books, p. 231.

4 Hemmington, N. (1999) 'Creating a culture of life-long learning at work'. *Continuing Professional Development,* Issue 3.

5 See www.saba.com/about.

1

Why All the Fuss?

Organizations have always been concerned about their competitiveness. Taking this seriously has meant developing the right products and services, recruiting and retaining the best staff, and keeping an eye on the future to ensure they are appropriately positioned to meet the challenges ahead. In the past this was a relatively simple task because the economic backdrop was one of steady growth and stability. This stability led to the creation of benevolent and paternalistic organizational cultures that looked after their staff and their careers. Employees could turn up for work in the knowledge that unless they did something very seriously wrong, they would be guaranteed a job for life. They were willing to place their future careers in the hands of their employers and, as long as they did a solid day's work and kept their noses clean, they would gradually move up the hierarchy over the course of their career. If they were very lucky they might even reach the board of directors.

Smart quotes

In a time of drastic change it is the learners who inherit the future. The learned usually find themselves equipped to live in a world that no longer exists.

Eric Hoffer

In this environment there was no real need for continuous learning because the workplace was predictable and stable. Learning was predominantly on-the-job and directed by the company, not the individual.

It is now clear that the nature of work has changed irrevocably and that the comfortable days of working with a single employer for 30 years and looking forward to a well-trodden career path are over. The business and economic environments are now more turbulent than they have ever been, with the long-term cyclical patterns in the economy being replaced by uncertainty and unpredictability. This turbulence and unpredictability is increasingly reflected in our working lives. We now have to contend with information overload, heightened insecurity, reduced job tenure and the loss of the incremental steps that defined our careers. In addition, the reduction in organizational hierarchies through downsizing has reduced the sources of power within the workplace, thereby making it more difficult to navigate through our careers. Consider the following facts about the nature of work:

- Our working lives are increasingly defined by what we know rather than who we work for and our position, status or title.

- The explosive growth of data is leading to information overload and an inability to maintain a sense of control over our working and non-working lives. Individuals now retain less than 20 per cent of the knowledge they require to be effective in their jobs. Compare this to the 70 per cent they were able to retain in the 1990s.[1]

- No employer can guarantee a job for life.

- Working life for the white-collar worker increasingly resembles an industrial age sweatshop with long hours, less pay and fewer benefits. This change is being caused by the combined effects of globalization, the aging of the West's populations and the effects of technology.

- The valuable jobs of the future will be those that involve the manipulation of knowledge. These will be well paid. Those jobs not directly associated with the knowledge industries will become increasingly commoditized with reduced benefits.

- Average job tenure in United States firms has fallen from 23 years between 1950 and 1960 to 2–2.5 years today.

- The average worker will have five different employers during the course of their career. This has forced employees to think more carefully about who they work for and what they want out of working life. It has also forced employers to think about how they can retain their brightest and most productive staff. <u>You would not have heard the term 'talent management' five years ago.</u>

- Shorter product life cycles are forcing organizations to routinely redefine the skills and competencies of their employees.

- Globalization is allowing organizations to develop and deliver their products and services using cheaper labour available elsewhere in the world. Increasingly, developing countries are able to compete with the industrialized world with very well-educated people at a significantly reduced cost.

Smart quotes

The whole game is moving to a higher level. So there is a growing premium on people, at all ends of the skill spectrum, who can work smarter, faster and better. You want people to be innovative (within guidelines) passionate (within reason), and armed with sufficient discretion to make mistakes (as long as they are not too big). Demand for those people is going to outpace supply for the foreseeable future

Bruce Tulgan

AVON

Avon, the beauty products company, is transferring its manufacturing capability from the United Kingdom to Poland. After 40 years of production, the plant at Northampton will be closed and its 465 employees will lose their jobs. Avon cite the tough nature of the global economy for the move and the growing market in former Soviet bloc countries. With Polish wages 30 per cent of the United Kingdom's, it's no wonder that the move will reduce production costs by 50 per cent.

With this backdrop of increased complexity and turbulence, organizations are recognizing that their staff need to take control of their own careers. Staff can no longer rely on their employer to manage their careers for them. Nor can they expect employers to retain them when their skills or performance deteriorate. Increasingly, employers look for continuous improvements in performance, productivity and adaptability in their staff, and some, such as General Electric will regularly remove their poorest performers from the payroll. Working life is no longer comfortable, and for many it is a fearful place in which they never quite know when the axe will fall. This makes work a miserable existence for all but the few at the top of the hierarchy who are cushioned from its effects (and even when they are removed from post, they usually have a huge pay-off). So what has caused this monumental change in employment patterns and what has lifelong learning got to do with it? Before we can answer the latter question we need to outline what has changed and why.

Globalization and technology have changed the game

Much of the change in the workplace has arisen from the combined effects of the globalization of commerce and the increasingly rapid advance of technology. One could not exist without the other. For example, the global

- Management thinker, author and guide through the fog of work.
- Author of the books *The Age of Unreason*, *The Empty Raincoat* and *The Elephant and the Flea* – seminal guides to the changing workplace.
- Predicted the changes that would occur within the world of work and how these would affect us as individuals.
- Identified the rise of the '½ × 2 × 3 workplace' (half as many people in the core of the business, paid twice as much for producing three times the volume). In essence, fewer well-paid people doing very demanding jobs.

financial system depends entirely on computer technology to process the millions of transactions per day and transnational corporations depend on their ability to manage their business seamlessly across the globe. Computer technology has advanced considerably over a relatively short period of 50 years. From its humble beginnings, information technology (IT) has become the most critical component in the smooth running of most industries and has fundamentally changed the way we work. Historically, computers started out within the finance department of businesses where they were used to process vast amounts of financial information, such as payroll and accounting. Computer technology was ideally suited to this type of processing and great tranches of manual activity were eliminated, although at this time staff were typically redeployed elsewhere within the business. The successful application of technology within finance demonstrated the benefits that could be achieved through automation. And it wasn't long before every function within the organization wanted a piece of the action. Before long, computers were everywhere and deeply embedded in the way work was executed. As a result, some jobs disappeared such as typists, whilst others were created, such as software engineers. Increasingly, we are all becoming familiar with the benefits and risks associated with IT. On one hand, it is unlikely that we can exist within the work setting without it and, on the other, it has the ability to reduce our career options. As we will see later, the implications on our working lives are significant and mainly weighted on the downside rather than the upside. For example, technology creates

Smart
answers to
tough
questions

Q: Will technology really have an impact on my working life?

A: Yes it will: just consider how far it has come in the short space of 50 years. The first ever stored program computer, BABY, was completed in 1948, and ran its first program in June of that year. This machine had a limited memory of 128 bytes, weighed one ton, was over 16 feet long, and required over 3500 watts of electricity to power it. The microchip on which the modern computer depends is 25 million times more powerful, and has 64 million times more memory than BABY. Clearly, the last 50 years have seen incredible advances in power, reliability, and price, and it would be reasonable to expect that the next 50 will see much the same. This will have profound impacts on our working environments and careers.

problems when systems malfunction, it displaces us from our familiar patterns of work and it forces us to cope with increasing levels of information and data. Technological change has shaken up the slow moving world of work familiar to the post-war generation and has created one in which business can be conducted at breakneck speed. It is this speed of change that has important implications for how much we need to learn throughout our careers.

We should be under no illusion that the advance of technology and its associated impacts on work will continue. Indeed, futurologists predict that by the year 2019, $1000 worth of computing power will have the computational abilities of one human brain – by 2029 this will have increased to 1000 human brains, and by 2060, to the collective brains of the entire human race. Perhaps artificial intelligence is not that far away. If it is, the world of work may no longer exist and we may enter the leisure society that was predicted when computers first entered the workplace back in the 1950s. The question then, would be who pays for it, and where will our sense of purpose come from? The transition may be too great for us to cope with because we have become so defined by work and the need to work, that a huge majority of us wouldn't know what to do with ourselves.

In tandem with the advance of technology has been the emergence of the globalization of commerce. The process of globalization started during the 1960s with the appearance of multinational and transnational corporations that coincided with the expansion of international trade following World War II. During the 1970s, a number of factors came together that moulded globalization into what we know today. These were:[2]

- The internationalizing of capital markets. The flow of capital across the world is now a 24-hour-a-day phenomenon.

- The expansion of international securities investment and bank lending, which has allowed companies and countries to fund their growth.

- The increasing sophistication of information technology used within commerce, especially communication via satellite and fibre optic cables. Companies can literally work on a continuous basis, effectively passing activity from one time zone to another.

- The emergence of the Internet. Despite the bursting of the electronic commerce bubble of 2000 and 2001, the Internet remains a significant business tool because it allows organizations to advertise and sell their products on a global scale.

- The economic competition from Japan. Since the late 1990s, the significance of the Japanese economy and its competition have reduced primarily through economic stagnation. This reduced significance is at least in part due to the aging of the Japanese population (see later in this chapter for the implications of an aging population on our working lives), as well as the mismanagement of the Japanese economy.

- The General Agreement on Tariffs and Trade [now succeeded by the World Trade Organization (WTO)] which heralded the beginnings of a truly global economy through the reduction of destructive protective government policies (taxes for imports and subsidies for locally produced goods and services) which reduced the flow of free trade across the world. The WTO, of course, cannot prevent trade wars from erupting from time to time, as we saw with the United States imposition of steel tariffs during 2002, but it is helping to keep them to a minimum through negotiated free trade agreements.

- The reduction in state control and the subsequent rise in deregulation. This has had a huge impact on the way transnational corporations have been able to dominate the global economy. Many are now more economically powerful than entire nations, giving them significant political muscle in respect of taxation, location and subsidies. Countries are increasingly offering attractive incentives to such organizations to locate their factories within their borders rather than someone else's.

- The oil crisis which brought into sharp relief the dependence on fossil fuels and the need to protect the local and global economies against shock events.

The impact of globalization on the flow of capital and the growth of world trade has been enormous. For example, the annual average percentage growth of world trade rose from 4 per cent between 1853 and 1913, to 6 per cent between 1950 and 1985, and 7.5 per cent between 1985 and 1996. At the same time, trade between companies has risen from 10 to 40 per cent.[3]

Each of the factors above has led governments and organizations to consider how they can remain competitive in a commercial environment with fewer controls and increased competition. Many corporations have responded by merging with, or acquiring, other organizations that are better placed to deliver a truly global service. Others have sought out the cheapest labour with which to manufacture their goods, leading to a massive reduction in the manufacturing bases of the industrialized world as the work has been transferred to the cheaper economies of the Far East, Central Asia and, more recently, China. With further advances in technology since the 1970s, globalization is increasingly allowing the transfer of knowledge around the world. And, with the emerging economies of Asia providing a ready source of well-educated cheap labour, corporations are beginning to source their knowledge workers overseas rather than at home. As the competition intensifies, corporations are having to develop more sophisticated knowledge-based products and services in order to compete within the global market. The process of globalization is therefore leading to an increase in the levels of uncertainty for us all, as it causes corporations to reconsider their hiring, location, and skill requirements far more regularly than in the past. It is also leading the uplift in the demand for smart, versatile employees who are capable of continuous learning. This is the upside of globalization.

GENERAL ELECTRIC[4]

In the early 1980s, when Jack Welch started to lead General Electric (GE), he decided to fix, close or sell every business that was not first or second in worldwide market share. He believed there was no other choice because the marketplace was increasingly filling up with foreign companies looking to steal GE's market share. The strategy resulted in the sale of over 400 GE companies and the fundamental restructuring of GE's business leading to over 170,000 job cuts in ten years. As expected, these changes also impacted GE's remaining employees. GE could no longer afford to be paternalistic and staff could no longer expect to have 30–40 years with the firm by keeping their mouths shut and working hard. They had to focus on continuously improving their skills, knowledge and productivity.

SMART VOICES

So, what are the implications of the combined effect of globalization and the rapid advance of IT? Five immediately spring to mind:

Smart quotes

… organizations and individuals everywhere are waking up to the fact that their ultimate security lies more in their brains than in their land or their buildings. Even in the beleaguered world of American auto-making, brains are replacing brawn. In Ford's new Atlanta plant, each car needs only 17 hours of direct labour. Clever workers with clever machines have put an end to the mass organization.

Charles Handy

1   None of us can be guaranteed a job for life.

2   The psychological contract between the employee and their employer has been severely eroded to the point where it no longer exists. No one should kid themselves when they hear those hollow words *our staff are our most important asset.* This is only true in times of skills shortages.

3   The world of work has become more pressurized, with longer hours, fewer benefits and more uncertainty.

4   The rapidly aging populations of the industrialized world are creating huge burdens on the state and these have to be funded by high taxation, which affects everyone in work. For example, the United Kingdom is having to increase the level of tax to fund the increasing costs of pension provision and healthcare. The demographic time bomb that has already hit Japan will be hitting the United States and Europe from 2010 onwards with major economic consequences. At the same time, the African and Indian sub-continents will become a major source of human capital.

5   Organizations are not around for long. Very few commercial entities survive forever, and many barely last beyond one or two decades. Takeovers, mergers, and business failures all take their toll.

Smart quotes

> In the past, many organizations operated in a paternalistic manner. Employees were assured lifetime security in return for loyalty and, in some cases, conformity to rigid rules. Over the past decade, most corporations have altered their policies, and fewer firms now guarantee lifetime employment …
>
> Robert Shaw

Let's take a brief look at these five implications.

No more jobs for life

In 1991, global unemployment stood at 800 million, by 2001 this had risen to one billion and, according to the international labour organization, almost 30 per cent of the world's population is now either unemployed or underemployed. As technology continues to replace manual and white-collar labour, the level of unemployment will undoubtedly rise and with it the likelihood that everyone's job will become more insecure. For decades, technology affected manual and blue-collar workers; office workers were mainly exempt. Not any more. The 1990 reengineering revolution stripped millions of office workers of their jobs, including many middle and senior managers – no one was spared. The increase in unemployment amongst the mid-career middle managers was largely offset, and hence invisible within unemployment statistics, by the return to work of so many wives, many, it has to be said, forced into work to provide some degree of financial stability. And despite the recent employment boom fuelled by cheap oil and money, turnover in jobs has never been higher and the nature of the new jobs created during this boom has changed significantly. More often than not, these jobs have been low-paid and part-time positions in the service sector, often called the pink-collar ghetto. Uncertainty within our jobs is here to stay and employers cannot offer any hope for those who desire long-term stability in their careers. Even Japan, which had always been held up as the employment model to us all, is faltering. Japanese firms are shedding staff and breaking their patterns of lifetime employment. Unemployment in Japan is now at an all-time high. Also, with the average job tenure declining from 23 years in 1960 to a little over 2 today, we should expect to change jobs many times over during the course of our careers.

KILLER QUESTIONS

How many times will you need to reinvent yourself to stay employed throughout your career?

As I write this book, I am currently working for my seventh employer, thus giving me an average tenure of a little over two years (as predicted above). Unlike those middle managers who were shocked to discover they were no longer needed and had failed to maintain the skills they needed for a long-term career, I have actively managed my own career, moving jobs deliberately and not relying on a single employer to guide me. This is the reality of work today, and key to succeeding in the new world of work is the ability to reinvent yourself. This depends on understanding what you need to learn to maintain your employability. It also means taking control of your career, directing your learning to expand your skills and capabilities, and recognizing that your usefulness to your employer will depend on what you do now, and what you can do in the future, not what you have done in the past. Increasingly you will only be judged on your last job. This, of course, is not easy, and something that fits uncomfortably with many people because it forces them outside of their comfort zone.

The end of the psychological contract

Previous 'revolutions' such as the industrial revolution only affected those whose livelihood depended upon their physical prowess. The coming of the information age changed all this and ensured the revolution was felt much

- President of the Foundation on Economic Trends in Washington DC.
- Author of more than a dozen books on economic trends, science, technology and culture.
- Provided a wake up call to the world of white-collar work in his book, *The End of Work*.

SMART PEOPLE
TO HAVE ON
YOUR SIDE:

JEREMY RIFKIN

wider than ever before. With the advance of the computer, the white-collar worker, whose intellectual abilities had been safe from previous disruptions in the job market, started to feel the cold wind of change. Great numbers of white-collar jobs were eradicated during the early years of computerization. As the process of automation continued, the level of uncertainty about longevity in the workplace increased. But it was the emergence of business process reengineering (BPR) during the 1990s that led to the most significant changes. BPR was designed to secure the long-awaited benefits from technology and make the corporation more effective and efficient with fewer employees. Initially starting within the manufacturing sector, it soon spread into the service, utilities and public sectors with dramatic effects. It wasn't long before BPR became synonymous with downsizing. As we have seen, the drivers that led to downsizing were principally associated with the globalization of commerce and the impacts of technological change. The fiercely competitive global economy led many organizations – particularly in the United States and the United Kingdom – to cut costs in response to the availability of cheap labour elsewhere, particularly in the Far East, China and India. And, given that the principal cost for any organization is its labour, it was this that bore the brunt. For example, between 1980 and 1993, Forbes 500 companies shed eight million employees.[5] And, despite the usually positive impacts on the bottom line such headcount reductions had in the short term, many organizations came to lament the time when they cut headcount with such gusto. For those that cut deep into their headcount, there has been a realization that downsizing has broken the psychological contract between themselves and their employees. As a result, organizations can no longer depend on their staff being more committed to the organization than to themselves. And for many, this has resulted in poorer financial performance, plus a general lack of loyalty to the firm. Moreover, there is plenty of evidence from corporate America that downsizing has worsened company performance rather than enhanced it. For example, in one study of 531 large corporations, more than three quarters had cut their payrolls. Of these:

- 55 per cent sought higher profits, but only 46 per cent of these achieved any increase at all.

- 58 per cent sought higher productivity, but only 34 per cent of these managed even a small increase.

- 61 per cent wanted to improve customer service, but only 31 per cent of these actually did.

- Within one year following the cuts, more than a half of those surveyed had re-filled the axed positions.[6]

It is also believed that downsizing has destroyed much of the cultural glue that held organizations together. It is ironic that many are now trying to re-establish what has been destroyed. Downsizing has resulted in the contract between employer and employee becoming too one-sided. For example, instead of being balanced with the employer offering security in exchange for commitment and responsiveness, it has become one-sided, with the employer still expecting commitment and flexibility, but only offering insecurity in return.[7] Furthermore, in times of tight employment markets, particularly within professional service firms (which bore the brunt of the headcount reductions during the 1990s), staff are more likely to change jobs than remain with their current employer. What is more worrying is that such one-sidedness means that employees are generally less committed to their employer and are no longer willing to go that extra mile. This can

One aspect is fairly clear: traditional loyalty to a company is a thing of the past. In its place self-interest will dominate. If an employer cannot be trusted to look out for an employee's welfare (can any employers promise that today?), then any self-respecting individual is going to look out for number one. If this means pursuing other job and career opportunities, so be it. Better to jump first than to be victimised by an unexpected layoff.

Terrence Deal and Allan Kennedy

Smart quotes

have a significant impact on the bottom line because employees turn up for work, switch off and do the bare minimum to get the job done. This is not unique to Anglo Saxon companies, as similar problems are now appearing in the Far East especially Japan. A final problem with downsizing is that it reduces the confidence of the staff. It is well known that those people who are concerned about their job tenure tend to be less productive than those who are not. This is because they believe they have lost control over their working life, have lost faith in their managers and worry about their ability to get another job if they lose their current one. All of this serves to make the employee less trusting of their employers.

This loss of the strong bond between employer and employee has affected both organizations and staff alike. No longer comfortable and cohesive places that encouraged loyalty and commitment, the environment had become one of fear and uncertainty with a culture of self-interest. Fear rules the roost for many employees; always looking over their shoulders to see if they will be the next to face the axe. Unfortunately this creates an atmosphere of distrust in which no one trusts management or their colleagues. Unwilling to speak out, drive forward controversial ideas or raise risks, employees are more likely to keep their mouths shut. This in turn creates a culture of self-interest in which individuals look out for number one, rather than remain loyal and true to the organization which employs them. Points scoring and backstabbing has replaced teamwork and honesty.

The intensification of work

Over the last decade the quality of white-collar work has gradually deteriorated for the majority of employees. The combined effect of technological change and globalization has resulted in a significant intensification of work. There are five issues that we all face in our working lives:

1   increasing hours;

2   job spill;

3   less time to unwind;

4   increasing stress; and

5   reduced employment benefits.[8]

Each issue impacts the next, creating a compound effect that has made people's working lives a mostly miserable experience.

Longer working hours are the root of the problem. For example, Americans are working longer and harder than ever before – 25 million now work more than 49 hours a week, with a large number working a lot more; 11 million spend 60 hours or more at work. The same is true for the United Kingdom which has the longest working hours in Europe; 91 per cent of British managers now work more than their contracted hours. Another study of working couples showed that almost half of men and over a third of women were working more hours than they wanted to. Downsizing has not helped either, as many who survived the headcount reductions found that their workload increased significantly. The increasing hours spent at

Smart quotes

Without work, all life goes rotten, but when work is soulless, life stifles and dies.

Albert Camus

the office is also reflected in the amount of work that is conducted outside of traditional working hours, mainly at home or on the commute home. Such job spill, as it is called, impacts our leisure time and invades family life. For example 39 per cent of Americans no longer take lunch breaks, instead favouring to work through to keep up with their work. In addition, commuting 'dead time' is becoming an extension of the working day, made possible by cellular phones, laptops and wireless links to the office. As expected, longer working hours both inside and outside of work mean that there is less time to unwind. With work spilling over to weekends and evenings, white-collar workers are finding themselves squeezed, with little or no time to unwind and recover from the working day. Worse still is that vacations too are being reduced through cost-cutting initiatives, reducing even further the time to recharge. With less time to unwind, workers are experiencing greatly increased levels of stress. Despite the impacts of job spill, longer hours, and reduced time to unwind, Americans are finding it ever more difficult to keep up with demanding schedules. According to the American Management Association, almost 50 per cent of Americans now feel stressed at work. Stress is a way of life for many white-collar workers irrespective of age or position within the corporate hierarchy. This stress is in part driven by the feeling of fear of losing their jobs if they are not seen to be keeping up.

The final issue that is creating an environment in which the other four can fester is the reduction in benefits from employers as they pursue shareholder value and seek ways to continue to drive up profits and please the investment analysts (although some of the ways were clearly at odds with the regulators, as we saw with Enron). Therefore, at the same time as expecting more from their employees, employers are scaling back the rewards they provide. For example, middle-income families in America saw their income rise by just $780 between 1988 and 1998. In the United Kingdom, companies are cutting back on pension provision, which is creating a pensions time bomb as fewer and fewer people have any hope of a comfortable retirement because they cannot afford to save enough money. The implications of

Smart quotes

Such deteriorating workplace conditions have already begun to produce palpable changes in the American psyche. As corporations practically boasted of their long-term commitment to employees during the past two decades – and prosperity's benefits were largely monopolized by top executives and professional investors – people of all ages and professions learned to replace traditional attitudes about hard work, just rewards, teamwork, and security with a new workplace ethos centered on cynicism, self-protection and a preoccupation with the quick 'score'.

Deal and Kennedy

this on the State, as well as on the individual are enormous. The State will have to bear the burden of the increased poverty levels within the pensioner community through the provision of benefits and safety nets. Individuals are faced with a stark choice of having to increase funding for their old age or work well into their 60s or 70s. So, for the majority, the misery of working life may well continue until they, literally, drop dead. Companies are also employing an increasing number of contingent and part-time workers as a way of reducing costs, and it should be noted that part-time workers find it very difficult to move into full-time employment. This locks them into a world of low pay, uncertainty and limited opportunities for career advancement.

Aging populations

The populations of the industrialized world are growing older. The bulge of the 1960s baby boom and the secondary boom that began in the mid 1970s and peaked in 1990 is hurtling towards middle age and retirement. At the same time, the average number of births per woman is falling to below replacement levels as women choose working life over family life. Consider the following statistics for the industrialized nations:

- In the United Kingdom, those aged under 18 will fall from 7.0 to 6.6 million between now and 2011. At the same time, the proportion aged 60 and over will increase from 12.1 to 14.0 million.[9]

- For ten years Germany's birthrate has been below the rate needed to replace its population. This will result in the population falling from 82 million to 59 million over the next 50 years and a third of the population will be over 65.[10]

- Japan has already reached an average age of over 40 and its population is expected to decline after peaking in 2007.[11]

- In June 2000, the OECD forecast that the ratio of elderly (those over 65) to those of working age (aged 20–64) would nearly double in the next 50 years.

- We will continue to live longer and longer. There seems to be no natural cap on how old the human race can get. Scientists believe that within a few decades we will be living well into our hundreds, not as the exception as is the case today, but as the norm. Even within the last 100 years, our life expectancy has almost doubled. This longevity will have profound impacts on how long our working lives will last and when we can retire.

It is clear that all industrialized countries are destined to experience similar problems as birthrates continue to fall. But it also seems that such falls in birthrate are no longer restricted to the industrialized world. Recent United Nations data suggests that the developing world is following in the West's footsteps, with families choosing to have fewer and fewer children in return for greater economic prosperity. With birthrates across the world expected to fall below replacement levels, the world's population is now expected to peak at 8 billion and then start to fall in the second half of the twenty-

New recruits are rather like greenfield sites – capable of much more efficient production to meet today's industrial needs – while older workers are more like long-established plants, difficult to adapt to new working practices.

Paul Wallace

first century. Some believe that the world's population will halve within 150 years. With this backdrop, companies will no longer be able to rely on a stream of fresh-faced twenty-something recruits to add to their existing pool of workers. Couple this with an aging workforce, and there are major problems on the horizon for organizations and workers alike. This is particularly acute when we consider how hard it is to change an older workforce.

Organizations will have to respond to this rapid aging by a combination of the following:

- Reconsidering the way they train staff as they grow older.

- Transferring their operations to the younger nations of the world.

- Tempting employees from overseas through immigration (such as the United Kingdom is doing to reduce shortfalls within the teaching and nursing professions). Mass immigration, however, requires political not just economic will because the numbers required are very large and the integration and social issues to be addressed are significant.

None of these are easy options. Training older staff who have become familiar with the working patterns of the past is difficult, especially as these are people who have not been brought up in the uncertain world we now live in. Moreover, it is unlikely that these people have trained themselves to continually develop new skills and adapt to new situations.

Equally difficult is how to transfer operations to the younger nations of the earth. Many have different cultures that affect their attitudes to work. In addition, there is an increasing perception that organizations that transfer work to other countries are merely pursuing cheaper labour in the pursuit of profit. Considering that the income levels of similarly qualified people vary by ten to one or more in real terms between rich and poor countries, it should come as no surprise that companies wish to transfer their operations elsewhere. Despite the benefits of relocation offered by developing nations, organizations have to contend with non-governmental organizations that lobby governments, pressurize companies and demonstrate in order to redress the balance between the exploited and exploiters. This makes it a much harder option to shift work overseas.

The final option of immigration is also fraught with problems. Immigration would have to expand well beyond the historical levels experienced either by the United States or Europe. For example, the European Union would need net inflows of well-qualified immigrants close to 20 million by 2030. Political will is vital if this is to happen and all indicators suggest that Europe and Japan will not allow such levels of immigration to occur (although they will be difficult to stop; witness the problems that the United Kingdom is having in preventing illegal immigrants from entering the country via the Channel Tunnel, and how difficult it is for the United States to prevent the mass illegal immigration across its southern borders). Moreover, it is essential to ensure that émigrés have the right mix of skills required by the economy. If they don't, they become an additional burden on the welfare state and an economic drag rather than a benefit. Because of the difficulties associated with mass immigration, it is expected that by 2030 the populations of Europe and Japan will fall 12 and 17 per cent respectively, creating problems for businesses everywhere.

Organizations: *they are not around for long*

It should be obvious that all of the issues identified above affect not only you but also your employer. You therefore need to accept that few organizations are around for long these days. Just as the half-life of information is reducing, so is the half-life of the organization. The reasons why organizations fail, are taken over or just fade away are manifold and include:

- Poor risk management. Many companies fail every year because of their poor management of risk. Headline failures such as Boo.com, the many other dotcom failures, and, most recently Enron, all point to the inability to manage risk. For those affected, it means having to find another job, and for some it means losing everything (as we saw in the case of Enron workers who lost life savings when the company and its share price collapsed).

- Takeovers, mergers and acquisitions. Whatever the reasons for mergers and acquisitions, there will always be some fallout for those that work in the organizations that are merging. Most mergers result in headcount reductions, often in their thousands. And within two years, most of the executives acquired during the process will have left, taking with them the intellectual capital of the firm.

- Bad management. Leadership is a major factor in the success or otherwise of an organization. Leaders who display poor judgement usually lead their companies to disaster instead of success. Being associated with businesses such as these is not good for your career.

- Inability to innovate and learn. This is increasingly a major factor in the gradual failure of an organization. The majority of organizations do not have the culture that permits innovation and creativity to flourish. They favour the knee-jerk and short-termist response and are unwilling to allow staff to take the risks they need to when innovating.

Unfortunately there are no magic bullets for long-term success apart from the ability to adapt, learn and change. Indeed, we only have to look as far as the Peters and Waterman classic *In Search of Excellence*, in which the authors linked the strength of an organization's performance to their underlying culture, and asserted that successful organizations shared certain common cultural characteristics. A mere five years later, only 33 per cent of the 43 organizations were still in existence. This outcome is supported by a study by Royal/Dutch Shell which found that between 1979 and 1994, 40 per cent of Fortune 500 companies disappeared.[12] So what does this tell you? First, that you can't rely on your employer to provide you with a safe working environment for your entire career. Second, that keeping your skills and capabilities as current as possible is essential so that if you are unfortunate enough to be caught out by a failing company, you will be able to find alternative employment in a short space of time.

Can you (or your employer) afford to be left behind?

There is no doubt that the preceding paragraphs make for depressing reading, but there is little point in pretending that the issues that these points raise will disappear. If anything, the combined effects of technological change, globalization and an aging population will lead to even greater changes in the workplace as firms attempt to remain profitable and, in many cases, viable. Although there are no easy answers, there is one common option that remains constant: human capital.

The ultimate survival of any business depends on the quality and abilities of its people. Equally, our individual economic health relies on our ability to add value in the workplace and to apply and adapt our knowledge.

Learning, and the ability to learn (and hence adjust to new situations), both at the individual and organizational level, are probably the best ways to navigate through the uncertain and turbulent future. At the individual level, failing to develop our personal learning abilities will lead to stagnation, unemployment and a career that will become a series of short-term, and perhaps part-time, jobs. This does not just apply to the basic office worker, it also applies to the professional, the senior manager and occasionally the board level executive. Old dogs, it seems, do need to learn new tricks. At the organizational level too, it is imperative to maintain an educated adaptable workforce, as to fail in this most basic of requirements will destine the firm to takeover or bankruptcy. Of course, this need to continuously learn is not lost on employers and is certainly not lost on professionals. For example, a survey by Watson Wyatt[13] asked top performers in their fields to rank the importance of pay, benefits, and other attributes. It found that professionals under 30 ranked career development higher than salary, and those over 30 still placed career development near the top of their priorities. Many organizations have also grasped the learning nettle by setting up their own corporate universities (see below). There is also a clear link between learning and improved productivity. For example, a ten-year study on work force quality carried out by the University of Pennsylvania found that a 10 per cent increase in education leads to a 9 per cent improvement in productivity.[14]

> Smart things to say about lifelong learning
>
> The more you learn, the more you earn.

Corporate universities

As the industrialized countries have transformed themselves into knowledge-based societies, the demand for new recruits with a higher level of education has increased dramatically. For example, 85 per cent of current jobs in the United States require education beyond high school, up from 65 per cent in 1991.[15] The traditional source of educated people, the universities,

All organizations learn, whether they consciously choose to or not – it is a fundamental requirement for their sustained existence. Some firms deliberately advance organizational learning, developing capabilities that are consistent with their objectives; others make no focused effort, and therefore, acquire habits that are counterproductive. Nonetheless, all organizations learn.

Daniel Kim

Smart quotes

have themselves changed to accommodate this demand by both catering for a much larger number of entry level students, and by offering more in the way of postgraduate courses, including masters and doctorates.[16] In addition, universities are now providing a much higher proportion of practical courses geared toward the needs of the workplace, rather than the generation of an intellectual elite.

But when it comes to lifelong learning, the key question that has yet to be resolved is who should pay the considerable costs involved. Should the public purse pay? All the trends seem to point to no, at least in the United Kingdom and United States, where those taking higher degrees in order to improve their employment prospects generally have to fend for themselves. And certainly those who work for themselves have to fund their own development, which at between £1000 and £2000 per course, is an expensive business. The demise of the individual learning account (ILA) in the United Kingdom is testament to the problems of who pays. The United States still provides a minimal level of funding, but this is just not enough to accomplish real lifelong learning. As for individuals, the costs for the majority are too high and help to limit the level of continuous learning that takes place. The advent of the Internet is changing all this. In the end, the bulk of the costs fall to the employer … as long as they see a return on their investment. Increasingly, the corporation is taking the matter into its own hands by turning to the concept of the corporate university.

UNISYS CORPORATION[17]

Unisys established its corporate university to help change the company to a services-driven, technology-enabled solutions business. This meant that they had to help their employees develop new skills that were very different from the technology-focused skills they possessed. The university is organized into eight schools, each of which serves a specific discipline: technology, e-services, leadership, sales, finance, HR/Legal, business, and marketing. Staff attend those schools that fit their individual career paths, which will include specialist as well as generalist courses. In order to reach all of their 39,000 employees, Unisys established a university in each of the five geographies where they have a presence (North America, Europe, the United Kingdom, Latin America, and Asia and the South Pacific). During 2001 they provided education to 24,600 of their employees. The university has been a major contributor to Unisys' success in repositioning the business and remaining competitive.

One of the first corporate universities was McDonald's Hamburger University, which opened its doors in the early 1960s. Since then the number of corporate universities has grown steadily as the need for lifelong learning has been recognized as a priority for most corporations. Growing from approximately 400 in 1985 to 1000 in 1995, it is believed that there are now some 2000 corporate universities in existence with an average yearly spend of $10.7 million.[18] It is now estimated that 40 per cent of Fortune 500 companies have established corporate universities, and at the current rate of growth corporate universities will outnumber traditional universities by 2010.[19]

Corporate universities have seven functions:[20]

1 Teaching corporate culture.

2 Fostering cross-functional skills.

3   Providing a central technology-based training facility.

4   Cutting training cycle times.

5   Operating training as a fee-earning business.

6   Providing education for non-employees.

7   Developing partnerships with universities and business schools.

Corporate universities are principally designed to provide timely training and education that has been tailored to the specifics of the organization. As a result, they tend to be practical, business-focused offerings that reinforce existing competencies and develop new ones. Typical subjects covered by such universities include corporate history, globalization, teamworking, quality, project and programme management, and leadership and leadership development as well as a host of functional subjects such as software development, sales and marketing, finance, and so on. The basic ethos of the corporate university is that all their workers should be learners all of the time and through this become effective organizational citizens capable of furthering the corporate mission. Many organizations are building on their experience of operating corporate universities and a small number are implementing more innovative approaches to foster learning. For example, BP Amoco is offering their employees guaranteed time to think and learn by providing them with personal learning days. Others are introducing life-long learning directors, directors of learning and similar roles.

So now you know that responding to the pressures created by the combined force of technological change and globalization is not easy for either the individual or the organization. But you also know that no response is not an option. Having a well-educated responsive workforce will make a considerable difference and will set the best organizations aside from the mediocre.

At the individual level, taking learning seriously throughout our careers will ensure that we remain attractive to those who employ us, either as full-time members of the organization, or as short-term contractors and consultants. Organizations too will benefit from a workforce that is keen to develop, learn and adapt. In addition, for those organizations that take this seriously, they will remain attractive employers to the talent that they need to remain competitive. Lifelong learning is, I believe, a virtuous circle where individuals gain satisfaction and long-term career opportunities and employers gain a smart workforce capable of tackling all that is thrown at them.

What can we conclude from all of the changes outlined above, especially in relation to lifelong learning?

- We must recognize that the ability to learn is an essential skill we all need if we are to cope with and survive the demands of the modern workplace. Charles Handy's prediction of portfolio work, if not already here, is on the horizon for us all. Organizations in the future will need people who are ready, willing and able to learn and change. Given that 50 per cent of all employees' skills become outdated within three to five years, the necessity for learning cannot be overstated.

- It is ironic that the majority of employees receive between five and ten days training per year when the half-life of knowledge is getting shorter. When we consider that the stock of human knowledge now doubles every five years, and by 2020 it is expected double every 73 days,[21] more effort is required from the majority of organizations to expand the learning expectations of their staff.

- Learning will be an essential ingredient to success, as will the ability to cut through the vast amount of information we have to deal with to remain on top of our jobs.

- Learning must extend beyond the obvious functional and technical skills and disciplines we have been used to developing. Knowledge work depends on other skills that are more socially based. Increasingly, therefore, we will have to learn coping, influencing, and emotional skills so that we can work smarter rather than just harder.

- Corporations are realizing that their very survival depends upon the skills, competencies and attitudes of their employees, and, more importantly, their ability to learn. Many are taking steps to help their workforces to learn.

- Policy makers are waking up to the knowledge economy and the importance of lifelong learning. This includes the OECD, United Nations and national governments.

Our futures rest with ourselves, and to survive the uncertainties we face in our working lives we must embrace lifelong learning. The rest of this book discusses how you can develop and benefit from a strategy that focuses on learning and realizing your potential. It begins by taking a look at how ready you are.

Many a man with the chemistry of a great ballet dancer spends his time dancing with other people's dishes in a lunchroom, and others with genes of a mathematician pass their days juggling other people's papers in the back room of a bank or bookie joint. But within his chemical limitations, whatever they are, each man has enormous possibilities for determining his own fate.

Eric Berne

Smart quotes

Notes

1 Hill, D. (2001) 'Keep it Simple'. *People Performance*, June, pp. 42–43

2 Jarvis, P. (2001) *Universities and Corporate Universities: The Higher Learning Industry in Global Society*. London: Kogan Page, p. 21; Hirst, P. & Thompson, P. (1996), *Globalization in Question*. Oxford: Blackwell, p. 18.

3 Langhorne, R. (2001) *The Coming of Globalization*. Basingstoke: Palgrave, p. 19.

4 Shaw R. (1997) *Trust in the Balance*. San Francisco: Jossey-Bass, p. 53.

5 Downs, A. (1995) *Corporate Executions*. New York: Amacom, p. 11.

6 Ibid., p. 12.

7 Reilly, P. (2001) *Flexibility at Work: Balancing the Interests of Employer and Employee*. Aldershot: Gower, p. 78.

8 Andresky Fraser, J. (2001) *White-Collar Sweatshop: The Deterioration of Work and Its Rewards in Corporate America*. New York: W.W. Norton & Company, pp. 3–74.

9 Source: the Henley Centre.

10 Buchanan, P. (2002) *The Death of the West: How Dying Populations and Immigrant Invasions Imperil Our Country and Civilization*. New York: Thomas Dunne Books, St Martins Press. p. 14.

11 Wallace, P. (1999) *Agequake: Riding the Demographic Roller Coaster Shaking Business, Finance and Our World*. London: Nicolas Brealey

Publishing, p. 3. Also see Wolf, M. (2001) 'Fighting for economic equality' *Financial Times*, November 28, p. 27.

12 Harris, J. (2001) *The Learning Paradox: Gaining Success and Security in a World of Change*. Oxford: Capstone Publishing, p. 12.

13 Plimmer, G. (2001) 'Yearning for earning relies on learning'. *Financial Times* – continuing professional development survey, December 3.

14 Bennis, W. (2000) Old Dogs, New Tricks. London: Kogan Page, p. 108.

15 'The power of the Internet for learning: moving from promise to practice.' Report of the Web-based education committee to the president and the Congress of the United States, December 2000.

16 Jarvis, P. (2001) Universities and Corporate Universities: The Higher Learning Industry in Global Society. London: Kogan Page, pp. 1–29.

17 Ibid., pp. 104–113.

18 'The power of the Internet for learning: moving from promise to practice.' Report of the Web-based education committee to the president and the Congress of the United States, December 2000, p. 8.

19 Trehern S. (2002) 'More than just a learning process'. *Financial Times* survey: Corporate Education, p. iv, March 25.

20 Chase, N. (1998) 'Lessons from the corporate university'. *Quality Magazine*, June.

21 DTI (2001) *The Future of Corporate Learning*. London: DTI, p. 6.

2
Are You Ready?

Having read Chapter 1, it should be clear that the case for lifelong learning is an obvious one with plenty of upside. But how should we respond? What can we do? With the half-life of information reducing year on year, we need to be smart at assessing what we need to learn and how we are going to learn it. Time, it seems, is of the essence if you are going to survive in these turbulent times. But responding to the challenge that lifelong learning presents is not an easy task because it requires you to take a long hard look at your capabilities, attitudes, and behaviours, as well as putting in the effort to make it happen. Success should mean long-term employability, more choices in your career, and employers clambering over themselves to have you in their organization. This may sound a little far fetched, but the changes in the workplace favour those who:

Smart things to say about lifelong learning

To learn now ensures you can earn later.

• change jobs more frequently;

- continuously develop their skills; and

- seek to stretch their capabilities and work outside their comfort zone.

The question is, are you ready for the challenges that lifelong learning holds for you? The following questions can be used to assess your degree of readiness for the road ahead. When answering the questions, choose the option that represents you the most closely.

1 *To what level are you educated?*

    a I left school without any qualifications.
    (b) I have non-degree level qualifications (high school, secondary education, or other non-degree level qualification).
    c I have a bachelors degree (BA, BSc).
    d I have a masters degree (MA, MSc, MBA).
    e I have a PhD.

2 *Since leaving formal education (school or university), have you undertaken any additional formal education?*

    (a) Yes.
    b No.

3 *If you were made redundant tomorrow how quickly could you find other employment?*

    a I could walk into a new job almost immediately.
    (b) Within 1–2 months, allowing sufficient time for interviews.
    c Within six months.
    d Not sure.

4 *How many times have you changed job in the last 10 years?*

   a Never.
   b Once.
   c Twice.
  (d) More than twice.

5 *How often do you review your skills?*

   a Never, I leave it to my employer.
   b Annually, when I am appraised.
   c Every six months.
  (d) Continuously.

6 *When was the last time you felt you were learning something?*

  (a) Yesterday.
   b Last week.
   c Last month.
   d Sometime during the last year.
   e I can't remember.

7 *If your job were advertised, would you get it?*

  (a) Yes, I would have no problem getting it again.
   b I might have difficulties.
   c I don't think I would get it.

8 *Do you know what you contribute to your current employer?*

  (a) Yes, definitely.
   b No, I am not absolutely sure – I have never asked.

c Definitely not.

9 *Do you know your learning style?*

a Yes.
b No.

10 *Do you see every challenge, success and even failure as a learning opportunity?*

a Always.
b Sometimes.
c Never.

Answers

1 *To what level are you educated?*

a = 0 (b = 1) c = 2   d = 3   e = 2

In a general sense, the longer you have remained in education the more likely it is that you will have been trained in how to learn. This is especially the case with tertiary level education because as a student you would have been expected to find out a lot of the information you needed to complete your studies, rather than have it spoon-fed to you as in school. In addition, university also exposes you to a learning environment in which the majority of students are self-motivated and are keen to learn. This again is very different from school, where many people are switched off from learning because of the way in which it is delivered or the way they have been brought up. In addition, schooling is a statutory requirement up to a certain age, so there is no getting out of it. These days it is important to have more than one degree. A first degree, although an essential entry-level qualification into

> Education's main value does not lie in getting knowledge, much of which will be obsolete sooner or later. It certainly doesn't lie in credits earned or degrees conferred. These may open doors of opportunity but only real competence will keep them open. In fact, in our rapidly changing world there is no 'future', no economic security in any job or situation. The only real economic security lies within the person, in his competence and power to produce ... Education's main value lies in learning how to continually learn, how to think and to communicate, how to appreciate and to produce, how to adapt to changing realities without sacrificing changeless values. Result? An inner confidence in the basic ability to cope successfully with whatever life brings.

Steven Covey[1]

Smart quotes

the world of work, will not set you aside from the increasing numbers who also have degrees. Having a second degree does, especially if it is relevant to employers. But you can go too far, as a PhD can be detrimental in some commercial environments. This is because it narrows the student's skill set to a very limited field and, unless this is something that is needed by the employer, it adds little additional value beyond a masters degree. A PhD can also make you too specialist to undertake any other role than that you are eminently qualified for.

2   *Since leaving formal education (school or university), have you undertaken any additional formal education?*

a = 3   b = 0

Many people are keen to continue their studies once they have entered the world of work. Very often this reflects the level to which they have already been educated. Thus those with bachelor degrees often want to gain a masters. Occasionally, you find that people without any formal education complete degrees later in life. For those who have nothing, the future is bleak.

3 *If you were made redundant tomorrow how quickly could you find other employment?*

a = 3   (b = 3)   c = 2   d = 0

This is a reflection on how employable you think you are and relies on you understanding what transferable and marketable skills you have. Knowing your worth is vital in the employment market of today. Clearly, if you don't know how long it will take you to get a job, then it is a good idea to check. With limited skills it can take up to a year to find other work. Anecdotal evidence from the United States suggests that the time taken to find alternative employment after losing a job is increasing.

4 *How many times have you changed job in the last 10 years?*

a = 1   b = 2   c = 3   (d = 3)

It is interesting how the perceptions of job movers has changed over the last 20 years. Previously, someone who moved jobs fairly regularly was frowned upon and considered untrustworthy. It was believed that such people had little loyalty and were unable to settle in one place for too long and were often viewed with suspicion. This all changed with the march of technology, globalization and, most importantly, the downsizing of the 1990s. Employees witnessed the destruction of the psychological contract and the rise of market forces. They recognized that their marketability relied almost exclusively on their skills and abilities, and what better way to enhance these than by changing jobs? So, today, the perception has reversed. People who stay in a job too long (say more than five years) and cannot demonstrate progression or significant learning are likely to be perceived as risk adverse, not interested in their careers, and inflexible. Such people may have become comfortable in their work and may not have taken the trouble to develop new skills, instead relying on their employer to re-skill them when required.

- Authors of *Blur: The Speed of Change in the Connected Economy*.
- Believe that our relationship with the market place is being blurred – we are no longer just employees, we are employers too.
- Asserted that the knowledge you have acquired over your career is a valuable asset that can be sold many times over.
- Stated that in the future, knowledge will become scarcer than money.

SMART PEOPLE
TO HAVE ON
YOUR SIDE:

STAN DAVIS
AND
CHRISTOPHER
MEYER

And don't fool yourself either by assuming that moving around a single organization is akin to changing jobs. It isn't. After all, you are still working in the same organization, you know the same people, and the learning required to become competent in your new role will be limited to functional skills only. Conversely, those who have moved jobs, reinvented themselves, and showed adaptability and flexibility are actively sought out. Recent research suggests that employees will have worked with ten different employers by the time they retire. Moreover, they will have probably worked in three different disciplines. Today's workplace requires such flexibility and those who have become comfortable with ambiguity and uncertainty and who have supreme confidence in their ability to continuously learn will be best placed to succeed.

5   *How often do you review your skills?*

a = 0   b = 1   c = 2   (d = 3)

Reviewing your skills, attitudes and behaviours is increasingly important. With the half-life of information reducing sharply, the knowledge you have come to rely on becomes almost worthless. The workplace moves on too fast to allow you to rest on what you learnt a few years ago. By the same token, you cannot expect your employer to manage your learning for you. Despite the rise of the corporate university (see Chapter 1), the process of skill replenishment is down to the individual. Continuously learning is an essential skill in today's workplace and those who rely on their employer or

SMART VOICES

ASSOCIATION OF GRADUATE RECRUITERS[2]

The Association of Graduate Recruiters undertakes an annual survey to assess what is important to employers of new graduates. The most recent survey pointed strongly to the importance of lifelong learning skills. This ability to continuously learn came only second to having good interpersonal skills. The picture that emerged from the survey suggests that employers now value those who are flexible in all ways, but especially in their willingness to learn.

annual appraisal to define their learning needs are missing the point when it comes to lifelong learning.

6   *When was the last time you felt you were learning something?*

a = 3   b = 3   c = 2   d = 1   e = 0

This really follows on from the previous question. Taking an active stance to learning means that you should be in a position to learn something, if not every day, then certainly every week. When considering this question, think about what you may have learnt over the past six months and what you expect to learn over the next six. If you are learning next to nothing it might be time to reconsider your position, as lack of learning may mean that your employer is not providing you with the skills you (and they) need for the future, or that you are not stretching yourself sufficiently to increase your abilities. As we will see, there are many ways to learn and pick up new knowledge. The essential ingredient is motivation.

7   *If your job were advertised, would you get it?*

a = 3   b = 2   c = 0

If you find it difficult to answer this then you need to consider what you need to do to ensure that you find it easier. One of the best ways to keep ahead of the learning game is to read the appointments sections of quality newspapers. These outline the skills and attributes currently in demand and provide an excellent opportunity to benchmark yourself against the job market. In these uncertain times you would do well to assess any differences between the skills and attributes employers are seeking and what you have, and feed these into your lifelong learning strategy.

8   *Do you know what you contribute to your current employer?*

a = 3   b = 1   c = 0

If you don't know what you contribute then how can anyone else? Although it is not always easy to know how we contribute, it ought to be possible to find out. Key things to consider here would be to understand how what you do improves the bottom line either by delivering better customer service and sales, operational efficiencies or productivity gains. Knowing this and then considering what skills and attributes you use to achieve these outcomes will help you understand where your strengths lie and, more importantly, where your weaknesses are.

9   *Do you know your learning style?*

a = 3   b = 0

Understanding how you learn is important as it helps you to get the most from learning situations. People tend to use one of four learning styles. They can be activists, reflectors, theorists or pragmatists. Activists prefer to use trial and error to learn, enjoy new challenges and like variety. Reflectors prefer time to organize their thoughts and like to watch and absorb information rather than leap into situations like activists. Theorists like to research new concepts and prefer structure to the learning process. These are people who enjoy complexity and stretching themselves intellectually with a complex idea or concept. Pragmatists like the practicality of learning. They want the application of the concept to a real world situation and tend to shun conceptual or abstract thinking (more on understanding how we learn in Chapter 4).

10 *Do you see every challenge, success and even failure as a learning opportunity?*

$a = 3$ $b = 2$ $c = 0$

It is possible to learn from any situation as long as we have an open enough mind. Unfortunately, we are generally poor at doing so for a variety of reasons. For example, organizational culture often restricts the opportunity to learn from experience because failure is frowned upon and feedback is generally ignored or rejected. This ensures that people do not rock the boat and that errors are repeated. Success also has the tendency to restrict learning because, as with failure, we do not take time to understand why we have been successful. Learning has to be an active process if we are to benefit.

How did you score?

0–10

You clearly have a lot to do if you are going to embrace the uncertain future ahead of you. You may feel that lifelong learning is not for you, and you may also have the feeling that the world is passing you by without any hope of catching up. But wise up you must, as any hope of a long-term career is looking very slim without some concerted action. You will benefit significantly from the contents of this book.

Another belief you may hold is that you know enough and that you really don't need to pick up new skills or knowledge. Wrong again. Such arrogance will not serve you well. I have found this in ex-forces personnel (especially officers) who move into commerce and industry after retiring from their military careers. They believe they know everything. In reality they know little of the real world of work and as a result add very little value in the short-term. Commerce is very different from the disciplines of military service. Such people expect to be obeyed and bark orders at those around them. They also lack content, expertise and appear to be unwilling to learn.

11–20

You probably understand the importance of learning and its link to your career and earning power. You are probably well-educated (to degree level) and may think that that's enough. You may also believe that the pursuit of learning predominantly resides with your employer and not with you.

Although your position is not as precarious as those who have scored 10 or less, your future will still be uncertain, especially as the speed of change increases and what you are expected to know and apply is in a constant state of flux. Taking a more active stance with regards to learning and developing a lifelong learning strategy (see Chapter 6) will allow you to take control.

21–30

You have a healthy attitude to learning and recognize the importance of learning and reinvention to your career. You probably take active steps to increase and extend

> *Smart quotes*
>
> Throughout our lives we use only a fraction of our thinking ability. We could without any difficulty whatever, learn forty languages, memorize a set of encyclopaedias from A to Z, and complete the required courses of a dozen colleges.
>
> Ivan Yerfremov

your knowledge through a variety of channels. This resource can be used to refine your lifelong learning strategy and enhance your already positive approach to learning.

Knowing where you stand, based upon your score, is one thing, but in order to derive the most benefit from assessing your readiness you need to:

- Recognize and overcome your learning obstacles.

- Ask yourself why anyone would want to employ you.

- Determine how you set yourself aside from your competition by branding yourself.

- Understand how you can future proof your career.

Recognize and overcome your learning obstacles

The painful reason why so many people fail to continue to learn and develop their skills is because they do not think it is worth it. But according to Dennis Waitley, author of *Seeds of Greatness,* it is because they are too lazy to make the effort. He believes that people have an aversion to doing more than is absolutely necessary to get by. The quiz you have just completed will test your attitude towards learning and if your score is low it may reflect the need to update your mental models associated with learning. Peter Senge, in his book *The Fifth Discipline,* describes a number of learning obstacles that reduce our ability to learn and you might want to assess which of the following applies to you.

- I am my position. This refers to the way we become defined by our job and how it can be very difficult to do anything else or think outside the confines of our immediate role. This tends to be reinforced by the culture of the individual functions people work within and the technical training they receive. In extreme cases this can be perpetuated as people move up the organization. For example, if we consider most career routes, they tend to remain within a single discipline, such as finance or information technology. This can act as a major barrier to learning and lead to blind spots in knowledge. In particular, such blind spots tend to arise at times of crisis when stress and anxiety prevent learning (this is an automatic, physiological response of the brain, which shuts down the reasoning capability in favour of a fight or flight response).

- The enemy is out there. This is a by-product of 'I am my position' and is associated with blaming others when things go wrong. This is very common in organizations where one function blames another when a project, product or process fails. We become so embroiled in our narrowly focused roles that we fail to see the wider issues involved. As a result, we fail to learn from the experience or see the other function's or person's perspective. This ensures that we end up repeating the same mistakes time and time again. In addition, too many organizations have a blame culture that prevents learning when things go wrong. As a result, people fail to take risks because the implications of failure outweigh the benefits of going out on a limb. When things go wrong in such organizations, every effort is made to find a suitable scapegoat rather than directing energy towards the learning required to ensure the same mistake is not repeated.

- The delusion of learning from experience. Increasingly, and especially within work, there is no direct link between the actions we take and the outcomes that occur. And although we learn best from direct experience, this is rarely the case within the organizational setting. To address this we must seek feedback from those around us so that we are able to learn from experience. Being a small cog in a large wheel usually limits an

Smart
answers to
tough
questions

Q: Why is failing to learn like boiling a frog?

A: If you take a frog and gradually boil the water slowly, it will eventually die because it fails to recognize the changes around it until it is too late. Throw a frog into boiling water and it will try to get out as quickly as possible. Similarly, if you fail to learn, your career will gradually disappear but you won't realize it until it is too late. So the answer is … turn up the heat!

individual's ability to see the bigger picture and prevents learning. The increasing complexity of organizations is reducing our ability to learn from experience.

- We fail to see the long-cycle changes. With the pace of work speeding up and our obsession with getting things done at an ever-faster rate, we often fail to see the long-term changes. Indeed, we often dismiss them as irrelevant. This is causing organizations and individuals alike to dismiss the benefits of strategy and planning. But without strategies or plans, it can be very difficult to gauge the results of action and learn from the experience. Short-termism also affects the way people manage their careers and develop new skills. Long-term trends are not used to focus skill and knowledge need. This has to change. This issue of short-termism is the primary reason why Stewart Brand wants to create the clock of the long now (see Introduction).

- Inaction and the knowing–doing gap. We all suffer from knowing that we should do something but failing to do it. We all avoid difficult situations, and we are all guilty of procrastination. The same applies to organizations that skirt around problems or spend endless amounts of time discussing their underlying components rather than solving them. This type of inactivity fails us all, and even though many people know that lifelong learning is an important building block for their future, very few embrace it … they know they should do, but they don't.

Senge believes that those who are keen to learn (and hence willing to overcome their barriers to learning) must embrace five disciplines:

- Personal mastery. This is all about personal development that is directed towards achieving stated goals.

- Mental models. They should update their mental models by removing those that are outdated and no longer suited to the modern workplace, and adding new ones which are more useful. This can be done by testing existing mental models against the external environment and adjusting them as necessary.

- Shared vision. They should be open with other people by sharing knowledge, taking and giving feedback and so on in order to achieve things collectively.

- Team learning. They should work with others around them to widen their learning network and capabilities.

- Systems thinking. They should understand how their organization really works, including the political and power dimensions (this is Senge's fifth discipline: being able to see patterns and systemic relationships).

The problem facing all lifelong learners is to accept that the learning process is different from the learning we experienced at school and university. It is a shame that so many people have been switched off from learning by the process they went through during their teens and early twenties. Many

SMART PEOPLE
TO HAVE ON
YOUR SIDE:

WILLIAM
BRIDGES

- Business writer and consultant.
- Author of the best selling books, *Transitions*, and *Managing Transition*.
- Offered a route through the uncertain job market in his book, *Jobshift*.

KILLER QUESTIONS

How can I make my-
self more marketable
than my peers?

tend to see it as a formal event that is dry and not particularly enjoyable. Alastair Rylatt, author of *Learning
Unlimited,* believes that a wounded learner is no different from someone who has been physically hurt, and that
to improve their health requires effort to first, understand
why they have problems with learning and second, to make
them more aware of their motivations and learning preferences.
Chapter 4 looks at the process of learning in a little more detail
and this should help you to understand the process through
which you can learn more effectively and, hopefully, with more
enjoyment.

Why would anyone want to employ you?

Having made an assessment of your readiness and looked at your attitude
to learning, it is now worth considering what makes you employable. Considering your employability is a great way to understand what you need to
learn, where the gaps in your knowledge are and what you need to include
in your lifelong learning strategy, which I will discuss in Chapter 6.

Employers expect a lot from their staff. Pick up any job advertisement
in any quality newspaper and you will see that the combination of skills,
experience, attitudes, and behaviours expected by any quality employer
are extensive. Words like flexible, team player, blue chip/Fortune 500,
fast-moving, professional, global, business management, entrepreneurial,

Smart quotes

> The attention economy is a star system … If there is nothing very special
> about your work, no matter how hard you apply yourself you won't get
> noticed, and that increasingly means you won't get paid much either.
>
> Michael Goldhaber

leadership, change, and so on crop up time and time again. Of course, these advertisements are painting an ideal employee who may not exist in reality – even inside the employing company's own organization. When it comes to interviewing and selection, employers will be seeking the ideal, but will usually settle for a candidate who matches as much of this ideal profile as possible. But just imagine that you had all of the skills identified, you would certainly be in high demand and have the pick of any job.

KILLER QUESTIONS

What are the skills you have that employers really want now, but more importantly tomorrow?

Job advertisements provide an indication of what the market place wants now and in the near-term. You would be wise to look at these regularly and test your skills against them to highlight gaps in your capabilities. Naturally, this is

Q: What do bosses want from their staff?

A: A recent survey by the London Business School of nearly 400 senior managers[3] found that they wanted their subordinates to:

- Develop their interpersonal skills by being more sensitive, more politically astute, willing to listen more, capable of building teams, and more assertive.
- Get experience by running something because it gives them the insight into what pressures their bosses face.
- Sharpen up their image, including being professional, looking proactive, speaking with authority and displaying gravitas, selling themselves, and networking inside and outside of the organization.
- Act like a leader by giving clear direction, vision, inspiration and enthusiasm.
- Tell them what is being done, ideally in advance.
- Clarify where they are going by having a strategy.
- Provide accurate numbers, especially financial.

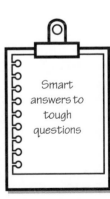

Smart answers to tough questions

not always easy because it requires that you take a long hard look at your abilities, and although it is possible to rationalize why your current skills are still useful, it is far better to consider which ones are no longer required and which new ones you need to develop.

These days, of course, it is not such a one-sided relationship with the employer calling all the shots. So, as well as making yourself attractive to your current and prospective employers, employers themselves have to take a more active stance when it comes to attracting staff to their firm.

The war for talent has emerged as one of the biggest management issues of the day, so if you have the right qualities you have the upper hand, not the employer. Despite the demise of the dotcoms and the recession in the United States and Europe, the war for talent is hotting up. It all began with the information age when knowledge replaced physical assets such as machinery and property as the key determinant of an organization's wealth. Look at Microsoft. Its continued success relies on the collective genius of its staff and nothing else. The fact that it grew from nothing to be the world's most dominant software company is testament to the shift towards the knowledge economy. Lifelong learning is at the centre of this new economy because without it, companies will not have the resources they need to survive. Even though the combined effects of globalization and technology are making for an unsettled working environment, the aging of the population is actually working in our favour – the pool from which talent can be sourced is reducing rapidly. For example, in the United States, the number of 25–45 year olds will decline by 6 per cent over the next ten years. This poses a headache for organizations that increasingly need to hold onto their best and most productive staff. But holding onto them is increasingly difficult because talented people change jobs far more frequently, especially the younger ones. A recent survey by McKinsey found that 20 per cent of managers expect to leave their company within the next two years, but 60 per cent more junior managers were expecting to do the same. Although high, this percentage does not include the large numbers of employees who would change their jobs if they could. A recent survey by the career consultancy Penna, Sanders and Sidney found that two-thirds of employees would change jobs tomorrow if they could.[4] These people are held back by anxieties over money, age or are too risk adverse to take the necessary steps. This same survey showed that nearly 20 per cent of people are not satisfied at work. With so many unhappy people at work, employers clearly have a problem as staff turn up for work and switch off. But more importantly, it shows that employees do not know their own worth or the talents that make them attractive to other employers.

Smart things to say about lifelong learning

If you know your talents, then it is easier to sell yourself to your current and future employers.

We have all seen people around us who appear to be more productive, produce consistently high quality work and effortlessly grasp new concepts and ideas. These people shine in the workplace. But in order to understand how we can become more talented, we need to understand what talent is. Knowing our talents also allows us to break through our mental barriers to realize our potential. Some of the techniques and skills described in Chapter 6 will help you break free from the anxieties that hold you back. Remember that lifelong learning is not just about the simple work-based skills we all need, it is also about finding out a bit more about yourself and developing a much better understanding of what you want out of your career. Life is too short to be trapped in a job that you find restrictive and unsatisfying.

SMART ANSWERS TO TOUGH QUESTIONS

Q: Is lifelong learning worth the effort?

A: With a war for talent in full swing, lifelong learning will provide you with the pick of the jobs. The effort will be paid back many times over.

Although talent is not easy to define precisely, it can be considered to be the combination of:

- knowledge;

- experience;

- intelligence;

- judgement;

- attitude;

- character;

- drive;

- energy;

- leadership;

- emotional maturity; and

- the willingness to learn.

KILLER QUESTIONS

Do you know what
your talents are?

Although not an exhaustive list, it does provide an indication of the qualities that are associated with talented individuals. I consider the most important of these to be attitude since it is this that determines how successful we are at developing the others. The good news is that these can be developed and enhanced through the application of such things as neuro-linguistic programming, which I will discuss in Chapter 4.

Setting yourself aside – brand you

I believe that long-term success in your career depends on how you set yourself aside from your peers. Understanding what makes you special, your brand if you like, is increasingly important as it defines your uniqueness and the mix of skills, attitudes and behaviours that make you interesting to an employer, or if you are selling yourself in the open market, your clients. Previous generations were defined by their position and job rather than their skills and attitudes. Daily activity, roles, responsibilities and work patterns were repetitive and predictable. This gave rise to the paternalistic organizations of the 1950s and 1960s. The impact of the computer, the energy crisis, the information age, booms and busts, and the advent of the Internet changed all this because it brought into stark relief the significance of the individual within the world of work. In particular, it was the shake up of white-collar workers during the 1990s that forced people to take more interest in their own careers rather than rely on their employers, who had long since dropped their paternal attitudes. Self-managed careers were in. Despite this wake up call, there are still plenty of people of working age who still just don't get the message. Thus, for those who do understand the significance, there is the chance to gain competitive advantage over those who don't. Branding yourself by understanding what you offer and then marketing it is probably the only way to set yourself aside. Creating a personal brand that is accepted in the widest possible sense means that you need to consider the following:

- Brand loyalty – how do you establish this?

- Brand awareness – how do you make your employer or client aware of what your brand means?

Smart quotes

… the war for talent is far from over … it will persist for at least another two decades.

Ed Michaels, Helen Handfield-Jones and Beth Axelrod

Smart quotes

… to be in business today, our most important job is to be head marketer for the brand called You.

Tom Peters

- Brand associations – how do you create associations about what you can do and how can you make those that come into contact with you instantly recognize what your brand means?

- Brand quality – how do you ensure that the quality of your brand remains consistently high?

Of these, brand loyalty and brand awareness are the most important. Brand quality is very much a component of brand loyalty, and brand associations are driven by a combination of brand loyalty and brand awareness.

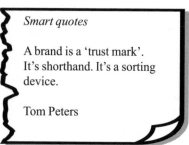

Smart quotes

A brand is a 'trust mark'. It's shorthand. It's a sorting device.

Tom Peters

Brand loyalty

Brand loyalty is all about how you are perceived by your peers, subordinates, bosses and clients. As with products, loyalty is a core dimension to your brand, as it determines whether people will come back to you for your input, direction and advice. Quite simply, this is because they have a consistent experience in every dealing with you. The advantage of brand loyalty is that is reduces the level of marketing you have to do to make you stand out from your peers. I believe that brand loyalty relies heavily on generating trust between you and those who you come into contact with. Ultimately, trust depends on how well you achieve results, act with integrity and demonstrate concern.[5]

- Achieving results. First and foremost, people trust those who are willing (because of their drive, discipline and commitment) and able (because of their knowledge, skills and courage) to deliver the results they promise. By contrast, we distrust those we consider misguided or incompetent. Anyone who cannot achieve the performance expectations that our organization imposes will be hard-pressed to earn trust.

- Acting with integrity. Integrity requires honesty in one's words and consistency in one's actions. People trust those who are direct in expressing
their views and predictable in acting within a known set of principles.
Inconsistency suggests that leaders are dishonest or self-serving. Those
who conceal or distort the truth, or who constantly change their strategies and practices, are rarely trusted. The impact of integrity is para-
mount early in a relationship, as each side assesses the degree to which it
can trust the other.

- Demonstrating concern. Fundamentally, trust requires that we understand and respect the interests of people at all levels and in all constitu-
encies. More specifically, people trust those who consider their interests
even in the face of potentially conflicting pressures. This does not require
people to place our needs above all others. We do expect, however, that
they will not deliberately take advantage of our reliance on them.

Brand loyalty comes from experiencing the brand, but before we can develop this, we must think about what we want our brand to mean and use
this to create our brand awareness.

Brand awareness

Making people aware of what your brand is, what it stands for, and what it
means in practice is essential and depends on your ability to summarize it.
An essential part of this is knowing about your mix of skills, attitudes and
behaviours that sets you aside from your peers and competition. We are
not talking about products, but individuals, so it is necessary to understand
your brand as a personality. Research into measuring a brand's personality
has provided us with some interesting dimensions to what people feel about
well-known brands. And although focused on products, these are equally
applicable to how we brand the people around us, and, more importantly,

how other people brand us. There are five personality factors that can be broken down into 15 facets and 64 characteristics[6] (see table 2.1).

Table 2.1 Brand characteristics.

Factor	Facet	Characteristic
Sincerity	Down to earth	Family-orientated, small-town, conventional, blue-collar, all-American
	Honest	Sincere, real, ethical, thoughtful, caring
	Wholesome	Original, genuine, ageless, classic, old-fashioned
	Cheerful	Sentimental, friendly, warm, happy
Excitement	Daring	Trendy, exciting, off-beat, flashy, provocative
	Spirited	Cool, young, lively, outgoing, adventurous
	Imaginative	Unique, humorous, surprising, artistic, fun
	Up-to-date	Independent, contemporary, innovative, aggressive
Competence	Reliable	Hardworking, secure, efficient, trustworthy, careful
	Intelligent	Technical, corporate, serious
	Successful	Leader, confident, influential
Sophistication	Upper class	Glamorous, good-looking, pretentious, sophisticated
	Charming	Feminine, smooth, sexy, gentle
Ruggedness	Outdoorsy	Masculine, western, active, athletic
	Tough	Rugged, strong, no-nonsense

When considering your personal brand, it is a good idea to consider which of the five factors and their associated facets and characteristics you want to display to your employer, customer or colleagues. The type of role you perform, or wish to perform, will influence the brand personality you will need to portray. So, if you are a marketing expert, it is likely that excitement and its associated characteristics will be of greater importance than ruggedness. Whilst if you are a project management consultant, it is likely that competence will be the overriding factor. This concept of personal brand can be used to drive your lifelong learning strategy by focusing on how you want to be perceived and then matching your learning and experience to achieve and reinforce the brand you wish to establish.

Smart quotes

If you can't describe your position in eight words or less, you don't have a position.

Jay Levinson and Seth Godin

It is important to recognize that developing your personal brand will take some time because you will need to take actions that communicate, reinforce and deliver your brand. Therefore, do not expect to have a brand defined and accepted overnight. Instead, understand what sets you aside, know what your unique selling points are and work hard to market your skills through strong delivery and reinforcement. Think about how you can develop a positive brand perception by getting involved with projects and initiatives that allow your brand personality to come through. Other things, such as writing articles, books, making presentations and networking also help you to communicate your brand. It should be clear that active management of your brand is essential.

Tom Peters believes that answering the following seven questions will help to focus your brand-related activities:

1   What are you known for now and what will you be known for next year?

2   What is challenging you, which might include your current project or role?

3   What have you learned in the last 90 days?

4   Who has been added to your external network?

5   What does your visibility (marketing) programme look like?

6 What you are doing to enhance your résumé over the next 90 days?

7 What have you done over the last year that has enhanced your résumé?

Future-proofing your career

KILLER QUESTIONS

What am I doing now to create a consist-ent personal brand?

The conventional wisdom of work and careers has been turned on its head. Stable working environments are a thing of the past, as are defined career paths. We can no longer leave our careers to our employer and we cannot begin our working life in our twenties and expect to be in the same career when we retire in our fifties or sixties.

Although much of what Super said back in the 1960s and 1970s still holds true, there is one major difference. This relates to the way we need to set and adjust our career objectives as we progress through our working lives. It is no longer possible, or indeed sensible, to set objectives that span thirty years or more, as it is likely that you will find

SMART PEOPLE
TO HAVE ON
YOUR SIDE:

DONALD SUPER

- The most influential writer on the theory of careers.
- Argued that working lives go through a series of five age-related stages:
  1 Growth (birth to 14), which involves building up a picture of the jobs we might like to do.
  2 Exploration (15 to 24), in which we build up a more detailed understand-ing of our interests, capabilities and values. During this stage we try out a number of job roles to help focus our choices.
  3 Establishment (25 to 44), which involves securing our place in our cho-sen occupation.
  4 Maintenance (45 to 64), which involves holding onto what career ground we have.
  5 Decline (65 onwards), which is where we become less involved and con-cerned about careers.

yourself unable to interpret or adapt to the changes occurring around you. Equally, having no plan is not an option because it means drifting through working life without any direction – something that employers just don't want. What we have to do is to plan our careers in three to five-year chunks. This allows you to assess how you are progressing towards your current objectives and then refresh these in light of progress and of the changes that are happening around you. Such medium-term career planning:

- Forces you to actively review your progress.

- Forces you to test the assumptions you have made about your career.

- Sensitizes you to the changes around you and their effects on your career objectives.

- Allows you reconsider your future more carefully.

- Ensures that you are taking proactive steps in the management of your career, thereby reducing the risk of your being impacted by a shock event such as redundancy.

When determining how to future-proof your career, you would be wise to consider the advice of William Bridges who wrote the book *Jobshift*. He believes that survival depends on the following three things:

- Your employability. Security comes from being attractive to employers. This depends on a number of things including your attitudes, behaviours, skills and abilities. It is important to recognize that your level of employ-ability will vary according to what is needed by your existing or prospec-tive employer. Learning plays an important role in this and, as we will see in Chapter 6, having a learning strategy that looks into the future as much as the present is essential.

- Thinking like a vendor (or perhaps like a consultant). Adopting this mindset allows you to determine how to add value to your existing and future employers by looking at the tasks you fulfil in a different light. It's time to stop thinking like an employee and begin to think like someone who is selling their skills and capabilities to a new client.

- Being resilient. In an increasingly turbulent working environment, being able to cope with what is thrown at you is vital. Flexibility, adaptability and a strong learning capability are skills at the heart of a long-term career. Things such as emotional intelligence and the skills related to neuro-linguistic programming (see Chapter 5) are increasingly relevant.

It is essential to change your mindset about your career and, more critically, understand that so much depends on your ability to learn and adapt. Being smart at spotting trends, acquiring new skills and knowledge, and dropping stuff that is no longer required is vital. This ability to unlearn things is an important part of lifelong learning and future-proofing your career. This is, of course, very difficult, especially if you have spent a long time developing the skills you no longer need. Going through a periodic reframing process is one way in which to identify those skills that are no longer valuable to you.

Can I do it?

The short answer to this is you have no choice. Your future career depends on your willingness to embrace lifelong learning and change tack in your career. Being prepared to learn means addressing the areas covered in this chapter and overcoming any of your inherent barriers to learning. Being open to the future and understanding the implications of the wider social, economic and demographic changes on your career will allow you to update your objectives more easily. The alternatives are bleak, with fewer employment opportunities, lower salaries, and less fun. Developing a trusted brand is another part of your armoury, especially one that demonstrates flexibility and openness to change. Employers are increasingly interested in those people who can adapt rather than those who have deep technical skills and experience, but are unwilling to change. The adaptable employee who recognizes the importance of learning is able to develop new skills and expertise in response to their changing working environment. Reinvention is critical here, and the lifelong learner knows how to achieve it. Nothing but ourselves stops us from reinvention and this depends on our ability to accept change. Being able to deal with change means a number of things:

- First, it means recognizing that change is inevitable.

- Second, it requires us to anticipate the changes ahead. If we do this, we are less likely to be surprised and we are more likely to prepare for it.

- Third, it means being able to adapt to change quickly, as sometimes action is more important than words.

The best way to summarize this chapter is with the model of Fig. 2.1. This links the future, work, and you. The future is determined by many things, especially the prevailing economic conditions, technological change and, increasingly, changes in the population and age structures within countries. Such changes define the types of work that will be available, the nature of the competition we and organizations face, and what can to be done to respond. Organizations usually have a wealth of tools and techniques with which to respond. They typically use a strategy and planning process to define and react to the future, utilize projects and programmes to implement change, and regularly adjust to the mix of skills they have within their

SMART PEOPLE
TO HAVE ON
YOUR SIDE:

SPENCER
JOHNSON
AND
KENNETH
BLANCHARD

- Authors of the best selling book, Who Moved My Cheese?
- Demonstrated the importance of embracing and enjoying change.

ranks through targeted recruitment and training. We, too, have more than we think at our disposal. Although we do not have the sophisticated processes available to organizations, we do have the ability to achieve similar outcomes by taking into account many of the things I have discussed in this chapter. The objectives we set, the brand we establish, the experiences we collect, and the learning we undertake are all linked. Our understanding of the future allows us to set objectives two to three years ahead, which in turn informs the brand we need to build and the experiences we need to have to reinforce and grow personally. Ultimately, all of this helps us to define out lifelong learning strategy. The important thing is to remember that the world is in a state of constant flux and we need to keep an eye on the changes that are playing out before us. Maintaining an external view ensures we are not caught out by the apparently sudden changes that occur in our workplace. It also allows us to evaluate the impacts on our careers and assess how we need to respond, particularly in terms of what we need to learn.

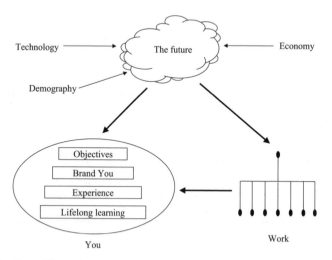

Fig. 2.1   Your wider environment.

In the next chapter, I will discuss the foundations of effective lifelong learning, knowledge and knowledge management.

Notes

1   Quoted in Harris, J. (2001) *The Learning Paradox: Gaining Success and Security in a World of Change.* Oxford: Capstone Publishing, p.19.

2   Kelly, J. (2002) 'New recruits must be keen to carry on learning say top employers'. *Financial Times*, May 8, p. 8.

3   Hunt, W. (2001) 'What bosses really want'. *Financial Times*, December 7, p. 15.

4   Overell, S. (2001) All present and correct in the comfort zone. Financial Times, November 30, p. 15.

5   See Shaw, B. (1997) *Trust in the balance.* San Francisco: Jossey-Bass.

6   See Aaker, D. (1996) *Building Strong Brands.* New York: The Free Press, pp. 137–174.

3

It's All About Knowledge

The shift from the industrial age to the information age has transformed working life. As we saw in the introduction, the numbers of people working in industries that require manual dexterity and brute force are already limited and continue to decline. It is unlikely that they will reduce to zero, but with the increasing use of technology within the primary and secondary industries, the requirement for low-skilled resources will continue to decline over the next 50 years. At the same time, the number of people who are employed in the knowledge industry or sectors that require data and information processing skills will continue to rise.

Smart quotes

Focused intelligence, the ability to acquire and apply knowledge and know-how, is the new source of wealth.

Charles Handy

The ability to succeed in the future world of work will depend on our ability to manage information and harness our knowledge as well as the knowledge which exists within the companies we work for. If this is the case, then the ability to learn is key. Learning involves taking our experiences

Smart quotes

These days, knowledge and information are what bind us together, and many people now earn their entire living acquiring and transferring knowledge or processing and handling information in one way or another.

Keith Devlin

and information and converting them into knowledge that can be packaged, applied and reused. Unfortunately, knowledge is nothing without information, so it is important to know what information is. Huge amounts of information are transmitted around the world every day, and millions of peoples' jobs are defined by the information they handle. Information can be collected, protected and exploited for personal gain. It is the very stuff of the knowledge economy and the glue that binds the organization together through computers, networks and the way we work with our colleagues.

Understanding the difference between data, information, and knowledge is essential. Data can be considered the atoms of knowledge. They are the bare facts that we see on balance sheets, in statistics, and in everyday life. On their own they mean nothing, because we need to interpret and add meaning to them. The process of making sense of data allows us to convert it to information. Information is more than the sum of the data because we will determine its importance based upon our own views and the contexts within which we work and are using the raw data. Therefore, looking at sales data and concluding that prospects are improving or deteriorating, or that one market segment is more profitable than another involves using data to create information. Information can also be derived from spotting trends and establishing patterns within underlying data. However, information is not knowledge. Creating knowledge involves combining more than one source of information to generate ideas, products and concepts or to take our level of understanding to a higher plane. Knowledge often becomes accepted as axioms, standards, received wisdom and is transferable through education and books. Thus, where as information can be interpreted in many different ways, knowledge is taken as the truth. This is not to say that knowledge cannot be questioned, reinterpreted or even changed, just that for many it has a value that is higher than information; a value that means it is not automatically questioned.

SMART VOICES

NATHAN ROTHSCHILD

On 18 June 1815, the future of Europe was in the balance. The Battle of Water-loo was nearing its climax. Two days later, Nathan Rothschild, the financier, met with one of his couriers at Folkestone who had just returned from conti-nental Europe with news of the battle. Hours before anyone else, Rothschild knew that Napoleon had lost the battle. On the way to the London Stock Exchange, Rothschild met the prime minister who had only just heard about the defeat of the English at Quatre Bas. When told of Napoleon's defeat, the prime minister refused to believe it. Then at the Stock Exchange, Rothschild sold thousands of Consols, which was the main government stock of the day. The price, which was already low, fell further as everyone followed Roth-schild's lead. Then, when the price had hid rock bottom, Rothschild placed one order for thousands of Consols. When the news of Napoleon's defeat reached the exchange, the price of Consols soared. Rothschild had used the information of Napoleon's defeat to great advantage.

The example of Nathan Rothschild shows the power of information when its implications are understood. Nathan took the information relating to Napoleon's defeat and combined it with his knowledge of the financial mar-kets of his day. Combining the two allowed him to benefit very handsomely. Every trader in every financial market uses similar skills, but today the time difference between when they know and when the rest of the markets know is much smaller because computers pump information around the markets in near real time. Wait too long, and the opportunity is missed, as is the op-portunity to make a profit.

Tacit and explicit knowledge

Knowledge comes in two forms. There is tacit knowledge and explicit knowledge. The former consists of those things that we find difficult to explain. It is knowledge that we pick up as we develop, as we work with

Smart quotes

There is no such thing as a
mind reader. It doesn't matter
what you think you know, it
only matters what you appear
to know. You are the only one
who can decide what is in
your head. You are the only
one who can let other people
think what is inside your
head. And what they think is
in your head, is automatically
in their heads.

Marc Lewis

colleagues, and as we navigate our way through our lives.
Think for a minute about the unwritten rules that exist
within your workplace. Such things as knowing how to
behave, who to avoid, who not to avoid, and how things
are done – all are tacitly understood. They are not written
down anywhere and they were probably not told to you
in your induction course. These are the things you have
picked up through observation, conversation, and interaction. They have been internalized by you and by those
around you. Similarly, there are skills you apply every day
that are deeply embedded within your brain, and experience that you don't have to question or revisit. You just
get on with it. The real advantage of tacit knowledge is
that it can be applied automatically and instantly; there is
no need to think before you act. When it comes to these
skills and capabilities, you are unconsciously competent.

But tacit knowledge can present problems, especially if it is wrong. It is also
very difficult to change, and, most of all, it is near impossible to communicate. This presents a challenge to us as we continue to learn through our
working lives, because we must unlearn what we already know and rewire
our brains to internalize new ideas, skills and capabilities. The only way we
can achieve this is to transform our tacit knowledge into the other form of
knowledge – explicit knowledge. Explicit knowledge is documented, held
in manuals, can be captured, searched, and reused. Our education taught
us how to collate and manage explicit knowledge, and during the process of learning, we began to internalize and augment this with our own
experience to create our own interpretation of the knowledge we gained.
Although many organizations have become very interested in making tacit
knowledge explicit through such things as knowledge management systems, many have found it difficult. Why? First, it is hard to formalize the
knowledge held in peoples' heads. For example, there was enormous inter-

est in intelligent, knowledge-based systems during the 1990s which could be used to subsume the knowledge of subject matter experts, such as doctors. The problem was that, despite hours and hours of questioning, it was impossible to extract every piece of relevant information used by the expert. Moreover, because the software relied on rules, themselves generated from the extracted knowledge, they were unreliable. Organizations also have the same problem. It is impossible to extract the collective knowledge of the whole corporation. Plus, as many have found, capturing, maintaining, and utilizing knowledge requires a lot of management attention, new software tools, processes, and, above all, commitment from everyone in the firm. A survey by the American Management Association found the main obstacles to effective knowledge management to be:[1]

- Getting people to seek best practice.

- Measuring the results.

- Getting people to share their knowledge.

- Knowing what to capture.

- Making knowledge assessable.

- Making knowledge usable.

- Keeping the relevant technologies up to date.

- Leveraging knowledge for competitive advantage.

- Determining how to use what has been captured.

- Finding the right people to manage the process.

What you tend to find is that there are usually only a few people who embrace the concept of knowledge management. The rest are not bothered. This is not belittling what organizations are attempting to do, but it requires a lot of effort, careful planning and commitment to succeed. Second, organizations and people in general are more likely to question the validity of tacit knowledge than explicit knowledge.

A good example of the consequences of questioning the value of tacit knowledge is the Challenger space shuttle disaster of 1986. Boisjoly, an engineer involved with the space shuttle programme, was unable to convince NASA officials of the dangers of launching the shuttle in low temperatures, when there was a risk that fuel could leak through poorly sealed 'O' rings. Without hard, documented proof of the risk, NASA refused to take him seriously. Then, 73 seconds after take-off, Challenger exploded. The cause? Fuel leaking through the poorly sealed 'O' rings. Boisjoly's hunch was correct, but without firm evidence he was unable to prevent the disaster.

The third problem with turning tacit into explicit knowledge is that we all tend to subscribe to the 'knowledge is power' frame of mind (see p. 87), particularly if we are concerned about our job tenure. Fourth, over time we begin to depend more on our tacit knowledge rather than on the available explicit knowledge around us. This may help to explain why resistance to change can be such a problem and why so few people actively learn. Despite these difficulties in transforming tacit into explicit knowledge, most organizations are able to convert at least some of the tacit knowledge into explicit knowledge and use this to create new products and services.

A helpful way of teasing out your tacit knowledge is to consider it alongside the dimensions below. A word of warning, however. Even this will not capture everything you know, but it will help to bring some of it to the surface, and hence help to make it explicit (at least to yourself).

MATSUSHITA[2]

Matsushita designed their best-selling bread-making machine by distilling the tacit knowledge of one of Japan's top bread makers. They achieved this through a long process of observation in which they spent days and days watching the bread maker perform his craft. Then, using this information, they created a series of prototypes which they tested and refined until the final product was complete.

- Know-how. This is the knowledge you use to execute your work roles. It includes the raw processes and procedures you apply and the techniques and tools you use (paper-based and electronic) to generate the outputs required of your role. Some of this may be explicit and written down in manuals, but the majority will be internalized tacit knowledge that you apply subconsciously as you go about your daily activities.

- Know-why. This is all about knowing the purpose of your role in the sense of the big picture. Many people work without knowing where or how they fit into the wider organization or economy. Understanding where you fit and what your role delivers to the business is key to understanding the value of your actions and your knowledge. This framing is useful because it not only helps you understand your current contribution, but it also allows you to identify what other knowledge you might need in order to make more of a contribution.

Smart quotes

The most valuable thing you have is your knowledge, which includes all the relationships and other intangible assets you've accrued over the course of your career. That's valuable to other people, too, and you can sell it. In fact, you can then turn around and sell it again, or sell it in a thousand directions at once.

Stan Davis and Christopher Meyer

- Know-what. This relates to the specifics of action, be they the detailed activities required to complete a given task, or the information needed to come to a decision. In essence, it is about data, either that which is needed to fulfil a process or procedural step, or that required to inform action or decisions.

- Know-who. This is the softer side to your knowledge. These are the people who you need to know in order to get things done. Know-who extends to relationships, contacts and, increasingly, those within your external network. Understanding who knows what within your network is vital and should not be underestimated. Having a network is one thing, keeping it alive is another. The good news is that networking provides additional opportunities for career advancement and a ready source of information and knowledge.

- Know-where. This is knowledge about where to find the information and knowledge you need. One of the most important lessons I learnt whilst at university was not what I knew, but where to find it. Knowing where to access knowledge (either your own, or someone else's) is a key skill. As we suffer from information overload, it is vital to cut through the sea of information in order to identify that which is important and valuable.

SMART VOICES

McKINSEY

Whereas many organizations approach knowledge management by trying to distil it into knowledge objects, McKinsey adopts a *Yellow Pages* approach. Here, subject matter experts are listed in a directory. So, rather than trying to develop and use knowledge objects, which usually involves reinventing the wheel, you can pick up the phone and ask an expert who can rapidly contextualize the knowledge so that you find it useful.

- Award-winning member of the board of editors of *Fortune* magazine.
- Pioneered the field of intellectual capital.
- Author of *Intellectual Capital: The New Wealth of Organizations*.

SMART PEOPLE
TO HAVE ON
YOUR SIDE:

THOMAS
STEWART

- Know-when. This is all about timing and judgement. In essence, it is about knowing when your knowledge should be applied. And although contingent on what you may be doing or the situation you find yourself in, it is surprising how much knowledge you can apply to similar situations. Never underestimate the power of judgement as this is built upon years of experience and the build-up of your tacit knowledge base.

Knowledge is power

In general, we all tend to hold on to the traditional view of protecting those things that have scarcity value. In the past, finding something out usually took time, effort and, in some cases, money. And because of this, it was felt the outcome of this activity was a personal possession. However, in the modern workplace, with so much information flying around, this type of mindset is outdated and counter-productive. Yet, we hear time and time again that people withhold knowledge that can be used to advance their careers or maintain their position in their organization. The start of this possessiveness about knowledge can be traced back to the downsizing of corporations that occurred during the 1990s. As well as the problems that delayering subsequently brought to the organization – such as increased

CORNING INC.[3]

In 1972, two thirds of workers used their hands and worked with things, today two thirds use their minds and work with concepts, data and information.

SMART VOICES

Smart things
to say about
lifelong learning

Information may be power, but it
can never become knowledge
without learning how
to use it.

costs, removal of the wrong staff, and difficulties in meeting client demands with a reduced and demoralized workforce – downsizing has had another side effect: the removal of some of the traditional sources of power within the once deeply-layered organization – typically status and position. This absence of power was soon replaced by another – information. If an organization is so dependent on its information infrastructure, then what better way to gain power than through the control of information? The shift to information power was probably going to occur anyway, but the downsizing of the 1990s accelerated it significantly. Holding onto information is now a very common behaviour and is damaging organizations' effectiveness. For example, a recent survey of the United Kingdom's *Times* Top 1000 companies revealed that critical decisions were being taken without access to vital facts because of the 'information is power' attitude prevalent in corporate culture.[4]

Managers jealously guarding islands of information is leading to decisions being made in the absence of the right information. The survey also revealed that these same organizations typically had computers on every manager's desk, and yet they often complained of not having access to the information they really needed. Clearly, the power that information gives is, like any other form of power, to be retained and jealously guarded, rather than freely shared. Another study found that 20 per cent of employees believe that it is not in their best interests to share knowledge, preferring to hoard it to win promotion, or move to another employer.[5] For those who develop new skills, advance their knowledge, and maintain their edge in their careers, this new power is a ticket to long-term career opportunities. For example, I know of contractors within the software industry who deliberately hold back knowledge to ensure they can stay longer with their clients. It is clear that holding back essential information is a sure-fire way of getting that contract extension and even an increase in daily rate.

The paradox of the information age is that sharing knowledge is power, rather than the other way around. Sharing knowledge need not be so traumatic, since when we consider the degree to which most of our knowledge is tacit rather than explicit, it would be impossible for someone else to know exactly what we know. Sharing knowledge has a number of benefits:

- Re-articulating what you know actually reinforces your knowledge and keeps it current because it usually requires you to revisit it.

- Other people can add to your knowledge and understanding by offering further insights and ideas, thereby increasing your own understanding.

- If you are willing to share what you know with other people they are more likely to reciprocate.

Ultimately, sharing knowledge is a collective process, where everyone in an organization is willing to take part. As a result, we all collectively learn, and the organization benefits. The key advice is to share your knowledge as widely as possible and maintain a network of knowledge sources. Holding back on your knowledge is increasingly a counter-productive mindset as it fails to demonstrate your capabilities and skills to your colleagues, managers, and employer. The bottom line is that you don't need to worry about sharing what you know because it is impossible to pass on every piece of knowledge you have.

SMART PEOPLE
TO HAVE ON
YOUR SIDE:

ANDREW
GROVE

- President and CEO of the Intel Corporation.
- Author of *Only the Paranoid Survive*.
- Recognized that Intel's future depended on the ability to harness knowledge and organization power.
- Took deliberate steps to break down the walls between those who possessed knowledge power and those who possessed organization power.

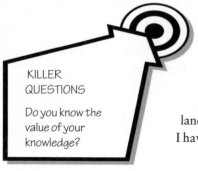

KILLER
QUESTIONS

Do you know the
value of your
knowledge?

Increasingly, information and knowledge are being used as political tools within companies. Andy Grove found this with Intel, and you have probably seen this within your own organization. So, part of your ability to manage your knowledge and the knowledge of those you need to tap into is the ability to understand and navigate the political landscape around information. Because this is an essential skill, I have included a section on politics in Chapter 5.

Generalist or specialist – which is it to be?

One of the questions you will need to ask yourself as you develop your life-long learning strategy is the degree to which you need to acquire specialist and generalist skills. The answer to this will depend on a number of things, including:

- Where you see your career five years from now and what mix of specialist and generalist skills you will need to fulfil your objectives.

- The importance placed on specialist and technical skills in your profession and workplace.

- How long you intend to remain at your current employer.

- What employer and position you will be seeking the next time you change jobs.

- Your current level of education.

The breadth of knowledge you need to accumulate over a lifetime of work depends on your chosen career path. It is clear that some professions require deep levels of expertise throughout, and hence for those that follow them, acquiring specialist knowledge is more important than acquiring general business skills. For example, there would be little point in a physician developing generalist skills when his or her ability to perform their job depends on their skill of diagnosing and curing disease. Furthermore, their ability to advance in their profession requires them to continue with their specialist education in order to maintain the currency of their knowledge. If we are to look at the job of a physi-

Smart quotes

We are moving from the specialist who is soon obsolete to the generalist who can adapt.

John Naisbitt

cian, the knowledge content of their work has increased dramatically. For example, when compared to the doctor of 100 years ago, the modern day equivalent has to understand microsurgery, antibiotics, ultrasound, x-rays and, increasingly, genetics. All of this requires continuous learning.

Even for those that follow a generalist career path, some degree of specialist knowledge is still required, especially in the early stages of their career. If nothing else, this provides a route into an organization and a selling point to a prospective employer. However, having established a foundation, the need to expand skills into other business areas is likely and usually expected by an employer. Therefore, for the majority of people, the requirement to follow a single specialism throughout their career is less important. Indeed, holding on to specialist skills for too long may actually become a hindrance to long-term career prospects. If, for example, you aspire to senior management, a deep technical background is not as important as a wide experience and knowledge base.

Whatever mix of specialist and generalist skills you decide you need, it is important to recognize that both require a lot of effort to develop. Whereas we may understand that the commitment required to become an expert in particular field is significant, we often underestimate how much effort is needed to follow a more generalist path. For example, consider how long

Markets are pitiless. They reward whatever creates value
and ignore whatever does
not. It's nothing personal.

Thomas Stewart

it takes to become a doctor, dentist, architect or engineer. Having spent between three and seven years at university, further study and professional exams are also required, which can take up to a further two to three years to complete. Even after that, reaching the pinnacle of a chosen profession requires continuous professional development and constant learning, often monitored by a professional body. Although this may sound like a long slog, the advantages of following a single vocation is that the path to the top is well-defined and the learning needed to achieve success is well-established. Also, for those who follow the major vocations such as medicine, dentistry, and teaching, there is unlikely to be any need to change tack in career.

From a learning perspective, adopting a generalist career would appear to be a much safer and easier path. But this requires more planning and the acquisition of a wider range of skills, as well as dropping those skills that become outdated. Think about your career so far. You have probably worked for a small number of organizations, worked in different functions and been involved with various projects. All of this has required you to adapt and learn new skills and capabilities. In a generalist career it is more important to have skills and capabilities that cover a variety of disciplines, coupled with one or two that are more specialist in nature. This has long been the view taken by consultancies who attempt to develop 'T' shaped consultants who have a particular specialism, for example supply chain, augmented by more general skills, such as teamworking, problem solving, selling and so on. This is important within consultancies because of the need for staff at all levels to sell, as well as deliver, assignments. The same principle should apply with your career, especially if you desire to move into senior management roles. Having skills that are more general in nature ensures that you can adapt more readily to the changes around you. Many people get caught out when the skills they have acquired and used over the years are no longer useful.

Organizations will often reassess the skills, attitudes and behaviours they need to remain competitive, and even more so in times of crisis. Recessions are usually the time when this occurs, and the 1990–1992 recession was a good case in point. The behaviours associated with the command and control organizations that had existed up until then were no longer valid. Out with tell-and-do and in with leadership and teaming. Unfortunately, many middle managers did not know how to change because they had not developed those kinds of skills. They were more comfortable with what they had grown up with and were certainly not used to working closely with their subordinates to get the job done. Inflexible attitudes and resistance to change led to the massive fallout within the middle management community. Many were devastated because they did not, could not, and would not understand why they were on the scrap heap. Those that survived were able to adjust, drop old skills and develop new ones; they learnt. Increasingly, skills associated with adaptability are far more important than deep technical capability.

Smart quotes

To create security, we must accept the insecurity that uncertainty brings.

Jim Harris

Tapping into the knowledge you need

We all need knowledge to survive in the workplace, but where do we get it from and how can we access it? This does not just relate to the knowledge that you have, it also includes knowledge you need from those around you. The one thing you have to become good at when it comes to managing knowledge is being able to seek it out and hoover it up. You also have to be good at converting your tacit knowledge into explicit knowledge so that it is more useful. This involves following a continuous process of making tacit knowledge explicit, updating it and then re-internalizing it so that it becomes tacit again. This not only ensures that your knowledge is kept up to date, but it also allows you to drop knowledge that is no longer valuable. This is very similar to how successful organizations manage their knowledge and transfer best practice to other parts of the enterprise. Accessing your own and other peoples' knowledge is best achieved through effective questioning. Unfortunately, we are all guilty of asking too few questions, and yet we all love to answer them. It is a sad fact that we often pay more attention to someone asking questions than someone delivering the answers. According to Dorothy Leeds, author of *Smart Questions*,[6] knowing when to ask smart questions gives you the edge in any situation. In particular, she believes questions help to:

- persuade people;

- gain information;

- plant your ideas into other people's minds;

- clear up thinking;

- motivate employees;

- solve problems;

- open communication between warring functions;

- overcome objections;

- get co-operation; and

- reduce risks.

In many instances, we fail to ask questions at all, even our most burning ones. And, once the instant has passed, it is often very difficult to ask for fear of appearing stupid. We should all take our lead from Lieutenant Columbo, who asked so many simple questions that he appeared to be a simpleton to his quarry, but he was always able to solve the crime and get his man.

Smart quotes

I keep six honest serving-men
(They taught me all I knew);
Their names are What and
Why and When
And How and Where and
Who.

Rudyard Kipling

Many people who struggle with the concept and demands of lifelong learning believe it is not for them because their current role does not require the acquisition and applica-tion of new skills. If you find yourself in this unenviable position, it is about time you sought out a new opportunity in your company (or outside of it if necessary). Apart from moving to a different function, one of the most effective ways of gaining new knowledge is to get involved with projects. Indeed, these days, what separates the mediocre from the star performers is not their position in the organization, but the complexity and value of the projects they work on.[5] As we have seen, titles matter less in the modern cor-poration. Far more important is the ability to demonstrate capability and build on experience. And, for those who want to enhance their skills and capabilities, one of the most effective means is through projects. Projects provide the ideal opportunity to:

- assimilate new skills;

- gain a better understanding of the inner workings of the organization; and

- develop the skills of an innovator.

Also, because projects are about changing the status quo, if you get involved with them you will gain invaluable experience of your organization, change management and innovation. They also provide the training ground for developing the vital skills of influencing, politics and stakeholder management. As organizations reinvent themselves over and over, they become more reliant on project management skills to do so. If you develop these skills, you will be in high demand.

Keeping it – maintaining your personal knowledge advantage

Let's be clear about one thing, maintaining your competitive advantage through knowledge requires effort. Your knowledge degrades very quickly if it is not used. It is a case of use it or lose it. For example, Motorola found that their trainees would begin to lose what they had learnt within 30 days if they did not apply their newly acquired knowledge.[8] Ian Robertson, author of *Mind Sculpture*,[9] highlights some very interesting research into the functioning of the brain. It is generally accepted that we use less than 10 per cent of our brain's capacity, but what we didn't know until recently was that our brain is shaped by the work we do and by our education.

Detailed post-mortems found that the more education someone had had, the greater the complexity and number of branches there were in the parts of the brain that dealt with language. The conclusion they drew was that education fosters the growth of the brain by stimulating the development of dendrites, the branches that connect the various parts of the brain together. It was also found that learning was not only good for developing your mind and your career, but it also protected you from the ravages of old age, particularly Alzheimer's Disease. This last point is supported by research from Italy which showed that people with no education were fourteen times more likely to suffer from senile dementia than those who had received five years of education. So, the next time you think that there are few benefits to lifelong learning, maybe you should consider how it can keep you healthy when you retire!

Ian Robertson also offers us some very useful advice on how to keep our memory (and hence knowledge) current. This involves linking what you are trying to learn to the things you already know. He recommends the use of the PQRST method as a practical way of achieving this. The acronym stands for:

Smart things
to say about
lifelong learning

Unused knowledge soon
evaporates.

- Preview. Before learning something new, form a rough idea of what it is about.

- Question. Ask yourself what you might already know about the topic, and any questions you would like to answer by learning it.

- Read. When learning about the new topic, do so actively by asking yourself the questions you have posed as your proceed.

- State. When you have finished learning the new topic, review it and attempt to relate it to the knowledge you already have.

- Test. Test yourself on what you have just learnt.

The good news when it comes to maintaining your personal knowledge advantage is that so few people bother to enhance what they already know. So it is easy to set yourself apart if you embrace lifelong learning. As more people wake up to the need to maintain their intellectual capital, the com-

Smart quotes

Walk in other worlds, look, listen, inquire, then go back and turn it into a new way of looking at your world, fix the new concept into your consciousness by using it. If it fails to make a difference, discard it, go look somewhere else.

Charles Handy

Smart quotes

As we enter the 21st cen-
tury, I can't overestimate the
significance of intellectual
capital. No organization will
remain in the phone book
unless its leaders address
the issue of how to generate
intellectual capital.

Warren Bennis

petition will undoubtedly increase, but for the time being there are plenty of people who just can't be bothered. I believe it is far better to be at the vanguard of the knowledge economy than with the laggards. First mover advantage is still open to many of us. All we need to do is to take it. Keeping it current then requires us to remain active in our learning activities.

Knowledge is at the heart of lifelong learning. It is also at the heart of our working lives. As the world becomes more knowledge-rich, we too must develop the skills associated with our personal knowledge and knowledge management. As we have seen, there are many dimensions to knowledge, and fundamental to us harnessing it is our ability to learn. The next chapter will look at how we learn.

Smart quotes

Ownership of physical capital, however, once the heart of the industrial way of life, becomes increasingly marginal to the economic process. It is more likely to be regarded by companies as a mere expense of operation rather than an asset, and something to borrow rather than to own. Intellectual capital, on the other hand, is the driving force of the new era, and much coveted. Concepts, ideas, and images – not things – are the real items of value in the new economy.

Jeremy Rifkin

Notes

1   Management Review (1999) 'Survey on knowledge management'. *Management Review*, April, pp. 20–26.

2   Leadbeater, C. (1999) *Living on Thin Air*. London: Penguin Books, p. 72.

3   Stewart, T. (1997) *Intellectual Capital: The New Wealth of Nations*. New York: Currency-Doubleday, p. 43.

4   Nicolle, L. (1998) 'Marooned by an island mentality', *Interface*, 4 November.

5   Fran, A. (2000) 'Staff hide skills from bad bosses', *The Times*, January 7, p. 11.

6   Leeds, D. (2000) *Smart Questions: The Essential Strategy for Successful Managers*. New York: Berkley Books.

7   Stewart, T. (1997) *Intellectual Capital: The New Wealth of Nations*. New York: Currency-Doubleday, p. 206.

8   Wind, J. & Main, J. (1998) *Driving Change: How the Best Companies are Preparing for the 21st Century*. London: Kogan Page, p. 277.

9   Robertson, I. (1999) *Mind Sculpture: Your Brain's Untapped Potential*. London: Bantam Press.

4

How We Learn

The breadth of lifelong learning is almost endless. We need to learn about so many different things that at times it seems too daunting and we don't know where to start. But the best starting place is understanding how we learn. Although as children we learnt things naturally, as we get older we have to develop and retain the skills of learning. At the root of lifelong learning is establishing some self-awareness about the process of learning so that we can develop our own learning style. In this way, it is possible to get far more out of the learning process and reduce the stress (perceived or otherwise) associated with lifelong learning.

Smart things to say about lifelong learning

Learning should focus on what's important now and tomorrow.

The paradox of learning and the circle of knowledge

It occurred to me a number of years ago that there is a paradox to learning

- Brought systems thinking into the corporate world.
- Author of *The Fifth Discipline* and *The Fifth Discipline Fieldbook*.
- An evangelist for individual learning and the learning organization.

that runs along the lines of the more you know, the more you don't know. This means that as you develop new skills, learn new capabilities, and so on, it seems that rather than mastering a subject, you have only scraped the surface; there is even more to learn. I have known people who are accomplished musicians or highly respected subject matter experts who believe they know very little. And yet, compared to me, or the average person they know infinitely more. It occurred to me that a circle could help understand why very knowledgeable people often state they know nothing, and why ignorant people say the direct opposite.

Try this test: draw two circles on a piece of paper, one small and one large. The inside of each circle represents a person's knowledge (everything they know) of a single topic, or perhaps all the topics they have a grasp of. The outside represents all the knowledge that exists in the world. The key part of the circle is its circumference, as this depicts how big the boundary is

Smart quotes

I was brought up on letters from my childhood; and since it was urged upon me that by means of them one could acquire clear and assured knowledge of all that is useful in life, I was extremely eager to learn them. But as soon as I had finished the whole course of studies at the end of which one is normally admitted to the ranks of the learned, I completely altered my opinion. For I found myself embarrassed by so many doubts of error, that it seemed to me that the only profit I had from my efforts to acquire knowledge was the progressive discovery of my own ignorance.

Descartes

- Published *The Hitchhikers Guide to the Galaxy.*
  - Handy electronic reference book.
  - Contains everything you need to know about the universe.
  - The ultimate learning reference.

SMART PEOPLE
TO HAVE ON
YOUR SIDE:

MEGADODO
PUBLICATIONS

between what they know and what they don't know. The small circle represents someone who knows relatively little. In this case, the boundary is small and as a result, there are few touch points between what the person knows and doesn't know. People with small circles of knowledge tend to be ignorant and arrogant, know-alls who think they have the answer to everything (or at least they have an opinion about everything despite not having a grasp of the topic under discussion). They live in a world of limited awareness of how little they know and don't feel motivated to learn anything new. After all, why should they when they know everything! Contrast this with the larger circle. Here, the knowledge boundary is much larger and the touch points between what is known and what is unknown are greater in number, hence the feeling that there is so much more to learn. Such people are hoovers, always seeking out new experiences or knowledge to update that which they already have. They are keen to learn and are usually natural lifelong learners. I believe that if you can motivate someone to expand their circle, you will find that as their circle grows they will want to find out more. In other words, they will develop the necessary self-motivation to learn continuously.

Understanding how we learn

Learning and the brain

The ability to remodel our brains is a latent skill that we all have. And in order to do so, you must engage in an activity that is unfamiliar to you. If you want to improve on your

> *Smart quotes*
>
> … our brains are wonderfully plastic throughout our adulthood. Brain structure is not predetermined and fixed. We can alter the ongoing development of our brains and thus our capabilities.
>
> John Ratey

existing capabilities, the same rules apply, although in this instance you have to engage in an activity that is related to the skills you currently have. John Ratey, author of *A User's Guide to the Brain*, cites a number of examples:

- Puzzles help to strengthen spatial skills.

- Writing improves language capabilities.

- Debating helps to develop reasoning ability.

- Networking with intelligent and interesting people enhances the general connectivity within the brain.

As you learn something new, the neurons within the frontal cortex become busy and so do many of their neighbours. This spreading out of brain activity is necessary to cope with the volume of input during the learning process. Once the neurons have fired together more than once, the cells and synapses between them change chemically, so that when one neuron fires it will be a stronger trigger to the other. This is called Hebbian learning (after Donald Hebb who discovered it). The amount of energy used during the learning process should not be underestimated and it helps to explain why we feel so tired when learning something new. The really interesting thing about the brain and the learning process is that with enough practice, the skills you learn become hard-wired. Hard-wiring in this instance involves the information you have learnt passing from the higher cortex to the subcortical area of the brain. This process is important because it releases the neurons associated with learning in the cortex to learn new things. This, along with Hebbian learning, helps to

Smart quotes

You can have the best imagination in the world with the brainpower of several Einsteins, but if you don't feed it, it will wither and die. And the great thing about feeding the brain is that it doesn't get fat and flabby and slow. It has a near infinite capacity for information.

Marc Lewis

explain why tacit knowledge is so automatically applied and requires little thinking when it comes to applying it.

Models of learning

Models of learning are designed to help us understand the process through which we pass as we develop new skills and capabilities. For the lifelong learner, the following seven models are useful:

- The four stages of learning (and unlearning).

- Learning preferences and neuro-linguistic programming.

- The multiple intelligence model of Howard Gardner.

- The Kolb learning cycle.

- Action learning.

- The DAMN cycle.

- The behavioural learning cycle.

The four stages of learning
When we learn anything, we typically pass through four distinct phases:

- Unconscious incompetence – we don't know that we don't know. We have yet to learn about a subject, such as driving a car or riding a bike.

- Conscious incompetence – as we begin to learn something, we are acutely aware of our failings and inability to master the skill we are trying to learn. This is when your neurons are firing within your frontal cortex.

- Conscious competence – we have begun to master the skill but still have to maintain our concentration and are still prone to errors. It is believed that it is during this stage we learn the most.

- Unconscious competence – this is where we apply the skill automatically without the need to really think about it. Your unconscious mind takes control, leaving your conscious mind to think about other things. This is where the skill has been hard-wired within the subcortical region of the brain.

The four stages model is useful for three reasons:

1   It provides a clear transition of how we move from knowing little about a new subject to mastering it.

2   It manages our expectations during the learning process by guiding us through the steps we have to go through and, more importantly, suggesting that it is not without its difficulties.

3   It suggests that there are some inherent dangers in being unconsciously competent, especially when we come to rely too much on our tacit knowledge.

This last point is important because operating at the unconsciously competent level allows us to develop bad habits and fail to change as the environment around us changes. Therefore, it is sometimes necessary to unlearn what we already know and relearn it taking into account the changes around us. And, because it can be very difficult for us to see the need to change, it can be beneficial to seek feedback from peers, or a personal coach, to help identify where change (and hence relearning) is required. This avoids the shock event where we suddenly find that we are no longer of any value to our employer. In this instance we can use the model in reverse in order to unlearn what we already know. This involves:

- Documenting the unconscious competence. This should begin by making explicit our hard-wired knowledge. This can be achieved by documenting what you know you about a particular topic, and having someone quiz you on it.

- Testing the conscious competence. Here, new information, be it research, personal observation or feedback from peers, is used to test the validity of the existing information about the skill or capability. In light of the new information, the current skill can be enhanced and updated.

- Reframing and relearning and moving back into conscious incompetence. The final part of the unlearning process is to begin relearning the updated skill. And, although not quite as painful as learning anything for the first time, it will mean being consciously incompetent for a time as you master the updated skill.

It is unlikely that you would ever need to move back into the first stage of the model, so it has been omitted. This model suggests that the process of learning is not without pain. Think about anything you have learnt, or when you started a new job. The first few weeks, and maybe months, were characterized by anxiety, a knowledge that you had a lot to learn, and plenty of mistakes. These were uncomfortable times. But after a while and plenty of perseverance, you reached a point where you broke through the pain and discomfort. This was the point when you moved from being consciously incompetent to being consciously competent and were well on the way to becoming unconsciously competent. This period was characterized by increasing confidence and probably some excitement as you finally believed you could crack it. Key to this process is persistence and having the courage to continue along the learning path. Many people, however, give up during the early stages of the learning process. If we had done this as children we would never have learned to walk. We need to rekindle the same courage we had when we were children, and break out from our tendency to make excuses when faced with something new.

Learning styles and neuro-linguistic programming

Neuro-linguistic programming is a relatively new concept that was derived from research into the transference of therapy skills between counsellors. The neuro (N) component of NLP states that our behaviour stems from the way we experience the world around us through our five senses. It also relates to our physiological reactions to the things we sense. The linguistic (L) element of NLP relates to the language we use to order our thoughts and behaviour, and the way we communicate with those around us. Finally, the programming (P) aspect of NLP refers to the way we, as individuals, choose to respond to the conditions around us. There are two elements of NLP that are of particular relevance to lifelong learning. These are understanding and changing beliefs, and maintaining peak motivation and performance. The former is about updating our belief system in order to become more effective.

As individuals, we all have barriers to personal growth that are embedded in the way we view ourselves, our capabilities and our abilities. NLP provides the basis for reframing ourselves so that we become more successful by focusing on our underlying belief system. NLP provides some tools with which to do this. These include modelling and visualizing success, reframing failure as an opportunity to learn, and understanding and adjusting personal values. The second element that is relevant to lifelong learning is maintaining peak motivation and performance. This relates to how individuals develop and maintain peak states by associating these with their physiology. This essentially means identifying physical feelings, body posture and mental images associated with success, achievement, and high performance and replicating these time after time. More importantly, it also means recognizing the physiology associated with low performance, and either avoiding it, or, having recognized it, switching into a more positive, high-performing state. This plays on the well-known fact that the brain's ability to process information is far greater when a person is in a high-performing state than when they are in a low-performing or anxious state. It also means that, when in a high-performing state, an individual is more resourceful and more able to overcome significant obstacles.

Neuro-linguistic programming has identified three preferences for the way we learn: visual, auditory and kinaesthetic. Visual learners prefer the use of pictures, models and graphs. They prefer to see the whole picture, rather than parts of it, so context tends to be very important when learning. Auditory learners prefer to learn in a lecture setting, as they learn more from what is said than what is shown. They value explanation and discussion rather than images or textbooks. Finally, kinaesthetic learners prefer more tactile forms of learning, and learning by doing. The kinaesthetic learner prefers activities and exercises that illustrate a point or help to reinforce what has already been said. Ideally, any programmes of learning should cater for all three modes of learning. We, too, should all understand our own preferences and ensure our learning matches our preferred style.

One of the key things about NLP is its link between the functioning of the brain and our physiology. Physiology is important and can dramatically improve our ability to learn. According to the latest research, our ability to master and remember, and master new things is improved by the biological changes in the brain brought about by physical activity. Physical exercise can result in better and healthier brains, which in turn will be better equipped to learn.[1]

Multiple intelligences

The notion that the best way to measure someone's ability is through their intelligence quotient (IQ) is gradually being eroded. And this has implications for the way that we approach lifelong learning. As the body of research grows that suggests that the most intelligent people are not necessarily the most successful, organizations are recognizing that all-round ability holds the key to success. And, if that's the case, we should develop all-round skills to maintain our position in the workplace. Howard Gardner of Harvard University offers a richer model that suggests that we all have a mix of nine intelligences:

- Linguistic – this is the ability to understand information in verbal and written form and includes the ability to tell stories, write reports, and critically analyse written material. It also encapsulates humour, wit, persuasion, and the ability to apply linguistic reasoning to problem solving.

- Mathematical technical – this is the ability to understand descriptions and instructions, and includes the ability to solve technical problems using the principles of scientific enquiry, logical thinking, and the ability to make objective decisions. It also encapsulates general financial skills and the basics of project management.

- Visual – as it suggests, this includes all things visual such as the creation of visual representations (graphs, presentations, and so on), a concern for aesthetics, and the ability to translate visual representations to the real world and vice versa.

- Auditory – this is associated with having a sensitivity for the dynamics of sound, and is typically found in musicians.

- Kinaesthetic motor – essentially a self-focused sensitivity for the physiological feedback from the body. It also includes the ability to use complex machinery and undertake intricate work.

- Interpersonal – the ability to accurately define the emotions and needs of others. This includes the ability to take into account another person's emotions and having the skill to adjust your behaviour accordingly. This intelligence, along with the next one, forms the backbone of emotional intelligence (see next chapter) and is one of the essential characteristics of a leader.

- Intrapersonal – the ability to know oneself in terms of goals, ambitions, feelings and emotions – also known as the inner game. This encapsulates coping skills, resilience, and determination, and represents one of the most significant checks for pure intelligence. Indeed, most very bright people lack this type of intelligence. The key skill of the intrapersonally intelligent person is the ability to reinvent oneself over time. Given the need to be adaptable and open to change, this is an essential skill for the lifelong learner. As we have seen, neuro-linguistic programming (NLP) provides the tools and techniques through which this can be achieved.

- Naturalistic – this is associated with the ability to relate to or profit from the natural environment, including its exploitation.

- Philosophical ethical – this refers to the ability to match your skills and abilities to different environments, particularly cultures. This would include being sensitive to different national cultures when working on an international assignment, for example (see Chapter 5 for more on cultural intelligence – an important skill within a globalized world). It also extends to having a sensitivity for the moral and ethical issues of a situation.

It is possible to assess where you stand across the nine intelligences using simple questionnaires and these will help you to determine where your strengths and weaknesses lie.[2] The beauty of this model lies in its ability to highlight your strengths across these other intelligences and prevents you from believing that intelligence can only be measured by IQ alone. Which, of course, it cannot.

The Kolb learning model

David Kolb's model is probably the most widely known tool for describing the learning process and determining an individual's learning preferences. Assessing an individual's learning style provides the basis for formulating learning experiences that allow the person to get the most out of the process. According to Kolb, the process of learning follows four steps that form a continuous, never-ending cycle:

- Concrete experience – as this suggests, learning from experience.

- Reflective observation – reflecting on events, considering alternative courses of action, and seeking out the meaning of things.

- Abstract conceptualization – formulation of abstract concepts and generalizations through logical analysis.

- Active experimentation – testing the implications of new concepts through deliberate action.

This model suggests that there are four types of learner that correspond to each of the four stages:

- Activists (which corresponds to concrete experience) – these are people who prefer to act rather than think in the learning process. Such people prefer to rely on intuition rather than logic, and prefer to learn in a real world setting rather than in the classroom. Trial and error is the primary method of learning.

- Reflectors (which corresponds to reflection and observation) – these are people who prefer to consider the pros and cons of things and like to take a lot of points of view and information on board before taking action. Such people prefer to learn through observation and from other people. Time is the biggest issue for the reflector as they need plenty of it within the learning process.

- Theorists (which corresponds to abstract conceptualization) – these people learn through abstract thinking and modelling rather than taking action. Theorists prefer to conduct research as part of the learning process.

- Pragmatists (which corresponds to active experimentation) – these people learn best by tackling a practical problem. They prefer to be given hints, tips and practical steps to success rather than researching it for themselves. They generally accept received wisdom at face value.

Action learning

The whole philosophy of action learning revolves around the simple premise that without action there can be no learning, and without learning there can be no action. The purpose of action learning is to provide an approach that allows people to self-learn based upon the application of new ideas and concepts. It also relies heavily on the ability to reflect on what happens when something new is put into practice. In many respects, it is all about feedback. Action learning involves three elements:

1   The introduction of relevant concepts, theories, models and tools.

2   The use of problems and simulations to test out the new concepts.

3   The inclusion of opportunities to evaluate progress, discuss findings and change tack if necessary.

Taken one step further, action learning can be broken down into five steps:[3]

1   Observation. It is essential that information is collected about what is going on around you.

2   Theoretical assessment. Having made your observations, it is then necessary to attempt to make sense of them by tying them together into a theory, or, where one already exists, mapping the observations onto it.

3   Experimentation. Any theory is of little value until it has been tested out. This is all about trying the idea out in the real world.

4   Audit. This involves assessing the actions and determining if they were the same as those expected from the theory.

5   Review. This involves updating the theory based upon the outcomes of the experimentation and audit stages. Such feedback is a vital element of action learning and, without it, the theory would remain fixed in the academic domain.

Action learning is believed to overcome one of the main problems with traditional forms of learning – the time lag between being introduced to new concepts and then applying them. In action learning, opportunities to practice are part of the learning process.

Smart quotes

One must learn by doing the thing; for though you think you know it you have no certainty, until you try.

Sophocles

The DAMN cycle

According to John Brown and Paul Duguid, authors of *The Social Life of Information*, learning is often treated as information delivery, training or teaching – essentially a supply-side issue – but learning is principally de-mand-driven; people learn in response to a perceived need. When people cannot see the need for what is being taught, they will ignore it or fail to as-similate it into their daily routine. However, when they have a need and the resources are available, they will learn quickly and effectively.[4] The DAMN model of learning recognizes this. The acronym represents:

- Desire – we all naturally possess the desire to learn and, left to our own devices, we will pursue some form of learning, although this may not be work-related.

- Ability – learning is not just about receiving information, but making sense of it. There is a need to put learning into action, rather than remaining a passive observer. According to Daphne Yuen Pan, lifelong learning requires the learner to develop an inquiring mind that will prompt them to question and search, as well as use higher order process skills that enable them to synthesize, evaluate, adapt and apply the knowledge they acquire.[5]

- Means – a solid infrastructure needs to be in place for lifelong learning to occur. This depends on both governments and corporations taking the lead and creating the necessary impetus and channels through which people can learn throughout their careers. The Internet is one of the best channels with which to reach a large audience, although it still needs plenty of development to make it world-class. Other channels include the corporate university, books, training courses, and so on.

- Need – the accelerated growth of information and the continuous change brought on by globalization and technological change should provide enough of a need. But the key driver for us as individuals is the desire to maintain our employability and skills. Ultimately, there must be some kind of push or pull to motivate people to learn. This might be the risk of losing out in the workplace (push) or the desire to progress (pull).

The behavioural learning cycle

The behavioural learning cycle is expressly designed to help us learn from experience rather than the traditional western approach to learning which typically involves being told what we need to learn and how we should apply it. There are six steps to the behavioural learning cycle:[6]

1   First, you need to exhibit the behaviour you wish to analyze and change. This might be how to deal with strangers, or how you might manage a meeting. Because this is situational, it may be necessary to either engineer the situation or deliberately seek it out in order to allow you to display the behaviours you want to assess.

2   Second, you need to be aware of the result that the behaviour elicits from those around you, or notice how it makes you feel. This requires a lot of sensitivity on your part, especially when observing how you feel, emotionally as well as physiologically.

3   Third, you need to reflect on the outcome, be it the response you received from a third party, or the feelings, emotions and physical response you noticed.

4   Fourth, you need to ask yourself why what happened did happen. This requires you to conceptualize the event and to understand the underlying factors that led to the outcome. In many cases, it might be worth referring to books that deal with behaviour as this will help you to interpret the outcome more effectively. This will then allow you to determine what alternative behaviour you might employ when faced with a similar situation.

5   Fifth, you need to apply the new behaviour and see what the outcome is. If it is better than before, then you have succeeded in addressing the behavioural change you sought. If further refinement is required, you may have to repeat steps 1–4.

6   Finally, you reinforce the change. In essence you have learnt the new behaviour.

The body of research into learning and learning styles is extremely useful for the lifelong learner for the following reasons:

1   It provides a frame of reference for matching learning to our preferred learning styles.

2   It allows us to develop a rounded approach to our learning by focusing on more than just intelligence – we are capable of developing ourselves across many dimensions, as Howard Gardner has demonstrated.

3   It gives us a process for learning.

4   It helps us break out of the fear-of-failure mindset.

5   It helps us avoid making excuses for not learning.

This chapter has reviewed the major models that describe the process of learning. All are relevant to the lifelong learner and being aware of what

SMART PEOPLE TO HAVE ON YOUR SIDE:

EDDY KNASEL, JOHN MEED, AND ANNA ROSSETTI

Believe the powerful learner is marked out by a number of characteristics:
- They are capable learners because they know how to learn.
- They are able to reflect on their experiences by standing back and taking stock.
- They are creative in the way they can look at problems and generate solutions.
- They are capable of asking excellent questions as a way of learning.
- They are collaborative in the way they learn – recognizing the importance of other people and what they can add to the learning process.
- They are capable of learning and working independently.

value they offer you as you learn is important. The next chapter looks at what lifelong learning should cover.

Notes

1   Ratey, J. (2001) *A User's Guide to the Brain*. London: Little, Brown & Company, p. 178.

2   Martin, J. (2001) *Profiting from Multiple Intelligences in the Workplace*. Aldershot: Gower Publishing.

3   Revans, R. (1998) *ABC of Action Learning: Empowering Managers to Act and Learn from Action*. London: Lemos & Crane, pp. 16–17.

4   Brown, J. & Duguid, P. (2000) *The Social Life of Information*. Boston: Harvard Business School Press, p. 136.

5   Daphne Yuen Pan *Lifelong Learning: The Whole DAMN Cycle – A Singapore Perspective*. www.apec-hurdit.org/lifelong-learning-book/pan.html.

6   See Ward, M. (1998) *Essential Management Techniques*. Aldershot: Gower Publishing, pp. 162–165.

5

What Should Lifelong Learning Cover?

Lifelong learning must combine the benefits of incidental learning with targeted learning. So, whilst it is important to have an open mind, it is equally important to plan your learning. And although lifelong learning can cover a very broad range of subjects, it is essential to cut this down to a manageable, but useful, subset. This is important because there is more information produced in one day than any one of us could hope to master in a lifetime. And without planning our learning, we face the danger of information overload and paralysis by analysis. Both are significant risks, which, if left unattended, result in limited learning and a tendency to give up. Therefore, as a starter for ten, I believe that lifelong learning should cover the following ten topics:

Smart quotes

The world is divided into people who do things and people who get the credit. Try, if you can, to belong to the first class. There's far less competition.

Dwight Morrow

1 Technology. We cannot ignore the importance of technology on our working lives, so it is a good idea to get to grips with some of the basics.

2 Business. Fundamentals of business and economics are a vital part of any ambitious executive's learning agenda. This increasingly requires an understanding of risk and risk management.

3 Organizations. Whether we work in them as full-time employees, contractors, or consultants, we have to be familiar with their inner workings.

4 Interpersonal skills. To succeed in our working lives we must be able to deal with other people. Working in teams is an increasingly important skill, as is dealing with people in general.

5 Intrapersonal skills. Knowing what makes you tick and what motivates you is as important as being able to work with others.

6 Emotional intelligence. This is another type of intra-personal skill that is increasingly important in the workplace.

7 Intercultural working. In an increasingly globalized world, it is useful to understand how to work in different cultures and societies.

8 Politics and power. If you want to get on, you need to embrace power and politics. So many people shy away from this and then wonder why they fail to progress in their careers.

9 Leadership. This is an important attribute whether you are leading other people or yourself.

10 Project management. Increasingly, the only way to implement change
in the workplace is through projects, and as this is one of the best ways
to learn, you had better understand what it involves.

As you will see from the list above, there is actually very little hard technical
knowledge apart from information technology and project management.
This is because we are generally good at developing our technical skills.
Organizations tend to be good at this as well, as this is where they can control the outcomes of the learning process more effectively. What we tend to
be poor at is learning about the softer side of work and yet it is these softer
elements that define how successful we are in our working life. Consider
those around you who you consider to be successful. What you will find
is that the majority are not technical experts. They may have access to the
expertise through their contacts, but they themselves will be more generalist
and adaptable. They are likely to be good at sensing organizational politics,
dealing with staff and colleagues, and will most probably display leadership
qualities.

Another way to view these and the other topics you may choose to include
within your lifelong learning strategy is as a series of four concentric rings
(Fig. 5.1). As the rings move out from the centre, they become more externally facing. Thus, the first ring is focused on ourselves
and the way we deal with our internal conversations
and motivations. So, things such as understanding what
makes us tick and what we want to achieve within our
working lives are important here. The next ring deals
with how we interact with those around us, particularly
within the work setting. Dealing successfully with other
people depends in part on how well we understand and
manage ourselves. The technical ring deals with all those
things we need to know during the course of our careers
and tends to focus on such things as technology and

> *Smart quotes*
>
> This philosophy of continu-
> ous challenge and continuous
> learning, which relates to our
> deeper desires, is growing
> with the demise of the tradi-
> tional notion of job security.
>
> Jim Harris

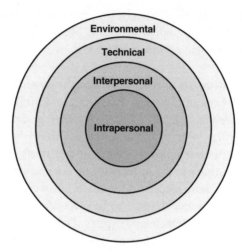

Fig. 5.1 The four zones of lifelong learning.

work-related skills and capabilities. The final ring, which I have termed environmental, is a catch-all for those things that we have to be aware of as we navigate our way through our careers. Here, such things as organizations, politics, general business principles, and the wider economy are relevant.

The key dimension of the model is control. As we move from the intrapersonal ring to the environmental ring, we have less control and influence over what occurs. In other words, we move from controlling to reacting, and hence risk management, behaviours. There are, of course, plenty of people who do not know much, if anything, about themselves who find themselves reacting to everything as a result. Life for them is akin to being in a pinball machine – lots of movement but no real direction. I would argue that it is imperative to know about yourself because this helps you to adjust to those things that you have less control over.

Regrouping the ten areas under these headings and expanding them to include key topics gives us:

- Intrapersonal: NLP, motivation, the inner game, emotional intelligence and Myers Briggs personality type.

- Interpersonal: teamwork, leadership, and organizational politics.

- Technical: technology and those technical skills required to complete your daily activities. This, quite rightly, can extend to cover a wide range of functional activities. Here I will focus on IT because of its centrality to most, if not all, businesses and project management because it is increasingly a core skill when managing change.

- Environmental: organizations, the international dimension, general business and economics, and risk management.

The purpose behind this chapter is to introduce these key areas as a way of whetting your appetite and building up your understanding of what things you might want to include within your lifelong learning strategy (which is the subject of the next chapter). It also starts to bring together some of the important areas within a simple typology (intrapersonal, interpersonal, technical, and environmental). I cannot hope to provide a detailed description of each of the topics identified, but there should be sufficient information under each heading to provide you with enough to be getting on with.

Intrapersonal

Life should be a journey of self-discovery and development. This depends on our ability to understand what

> *Smart quotes*
>
> Know thyself.
>
> Anonymous

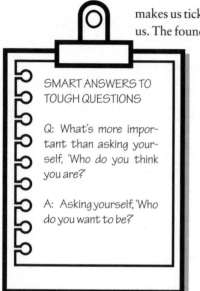

SMART ANSWERS TO
TOUGH QUESTIONS

Q: What's more impor-
tant than asking your-
self, 'Who do you think
you are?'

A: Asking yourself, 'Who
do you want to be?'

makes us tick, what motivates us, and how we deal with the events around us. The foundation on which success in our working life depends is almost entirely made up of how we manage ourselves. Lifelong learning must begin with understanding ourselves, as this allows us to interact with other people more effectively and deal with the uncertainties we face more readily. The sheer numbers of self-help books available today is testament to the interest people have in improving their lives by understanding what makes them function and behave the way they do. There are, of course, many areas which you can explore. But for work, I believe there are five: NLP, motivation, emotional intelligence, the inner game and your Myers Briggs personality type. In the next few paragraphs, I will draw out the salient elements of each so that you have enough to get you started and ideally generate an interest to find out a lot more about yourself.

NLP

The basics of NLP were introduced in the previous chapter including the basic tenets of the concept and their relation to how we learn. The discussion here relates to how we can use NLP to understand how to deal with the challenges we face in our working lives, and how we can develop more useful attitudes and behaviours when addressing them.

One of basic things that NLP teaches us is the need to understand the values that we hold about the various dimensions to our lives, including our careers, health, and personal development. Failing to assess these in detail often means that our actions drift out of alignment with what we value, which usually leads to dissatisfaction and a reduction in our ability to reach our true potential. Unfortunately, without gaining an insight into your values, you tend to see these as setbacks or problems brought on by those around you, which, in turn, ensures you enter a vicious circle that can

- Authors of *Breakthrough to Peak Performance*, and founders of Speakers International.
- Believe we are all capable of breaking though to our peak-performing state.
- Assert that peak performance is reached by developing skills in five key areas:
  - Personal leadership and taking responsibility for your future.
  - Mastering your motivation.
  - Harnessing the power of belief. After all, what we believe ultimately defines us.
  - Developing rapport with those around us.
  - Tapping into our creative communication by using our three channels (visual, auditory, and kinaesthetic – see Chapter 4).

SMART PEOPLE
TO HAVE ON
YOUR SIDE:

JIM STEELE,
COLIN HILES
AND
MARTIN
COBURN

be difficult to break out of. This is where the second important component of NLP – personal leadership – comes to the rescue. This is about developing a personal vision and sticking to it. When we think of some of the great composers (for example, Beethoven), writers (Leo Tolstoy, Louisa May Alcott), entrepreneurs (Henry Ford, Walt Disney, and F.W. Woolworth), and scientists (Thomas Edison, Albert Einstein, Charles Darwin, Isaac Newton, and Louis Pasteur) and look into their lives in more detail, we see that they overcame adversity and rejection to achieve great things. This demonstrates the power of personal leadership. Many people have a limiting vision of themselves and their environment which ensures that they fail. It also prevents them learning when things go wrong. Setting goals and working towards them, even when faced with setbacks, is the sign of a leader and someone who is able to motivate themselves.

Learning is another important dimension of NLP as it helps to frame failure as an opportunity for success. So, rather than blaming others when you fail, NLP teaches us to take responsibility for failure and helps us to develop a more healthy response that looks to solve the problem in hand rather than seeking someone to blame. In essence, NLP recognizes that the outcome of any event is completely dependent upon how we respond to it. If we respond in a negative way, we can guarantee that the problem will remain. However, if we react in a positive way, it is likely that the issue will appear less extreme and will be resolved.

What all of the above suggests is that the key to success in most things in our lives, and especially our workplace, depends on what goes on in our brains. The mental images, attitudes, and behaviours stored in our heads and the conversations we have (also in our heads – see 'The inner game' below) dictate how we motivate ourselves, how we work with others, and how successful, or indeed unsuccessful, we ultimately become. But, before we leave the topic of NLP, there is one final aspect that is also important and that is the link between what goes on in our heads and our physiology. As we saw in the previous chapter, learning can be greatly enhanced by combining it with physical activity. The same is true with our general performance. When we are physically fit and energized, we feel able to cope with anything that life throws at us. When, however, we are tired and listless, we don't feel capable of doing much else but sleep. The reason for this lies in how the brain works. The brain tends to shut down its higher order areas when the body is tired, as energy needs to be spent rejuvenating the body rather than dealing with other stimuli. In other words, it is unable to access all of its capacity. The opposite is true when the body is energized and active. Therefore, creating a physiologically positive state is one of the best things you can do when it comes to dealing with working life and, of course, lifelong learning. This is usually termed 'playing from a ten'.

Smart quotes

It is the mind that maketh good or ill, that maketh wretch, happy or poor.

Edmund Spenser

The inner game

The inner game has been popularized by Timothy Gallwey who developed the idea whilst a sports coach. Very simply, the inner game is about the internal conversations that occur within your head between what Gallwey terms Self 1 and Self 2:

- Self 1 is the stern know-it-all who issues commands and judges the results. This is the inner conversation that says, 'you haven't finished this yet' or 'I'm not sure if this is a good idea'. Self 1 is generally untrusting of Self 2.

- Self 2 is the human being itself. Packed with natural potential as well as the skills and capabilities to achieve most things. More importantly, it includes our ability to learn and grow.

Our ability to continue to develop and realize our potential depends heavily on our ability to limit the controlling Self 1 and to allow Self 2 to carry out the tasks in hand in a calm and natural manner. Gallwey noticed this during coaching sessions with tennis players and later with golfers. By focusing the judgemental Self 1 on a component of the ball, such as its speed, he found that a player's Self 2 would take over and make a perfect hit. Thus, turning down or distracting Self 1 was key to success in improving the game. This is similar to the state of flow that we sometimes reach when we are so focused on a task that time flies and we seem to tackle it effortlessly. Gallwey has since applied the concept within the corporate setting to good effect.[1] The inner game is an excellent way to interpret and ultimately manage your internal dialogue and, when matched with NLP, can be a powerful aid to the learning process.

> Rather than waiting for the world to give them what they want, people can become more proactive in making things happen for themselves. They can get the interactive process working on their behalf by behaving more autonomously. They can elicit from the social context more and more support for their autonomy. Their personality and social contexts in which they operate are synergistic and together they affect people's experiences and actions.
>
> Edward Deci

Smart quotes

Motivation

According to Edward Deci, author of *Why We Do What We Do*, self-motivation rather than external motivation is at the heart of creativity, responsibility, healthy behaviour, and lasting change. So, understanding what motivates us and why it does should be the foundation of lifelong learning. We are all used to the model of motivation that goes along the lines of, 'If you do this, I'll give you that'. Such extrinsic motivation drives behaviour in organizations and ourselves. So if your workplace offers bonuses, and these are based upon achieving certain performance objectives such as sales, you will focus on the small number of things that will generate the reward. The size of the reward will determine how much attention you give to those things that have no bearing on the outcome. The problem with this type of motivation is that it can restrict behaviours that are conducive to learning. The alternative to extrinsic motivation is intrinsic motivation, which is the desire to engage in an activity for its own sake.[2] To some extent, lifelong learning requires a combination of the two. It is impossible to argue that there are significant rewards to be had from embracing it, and equally it helps if you have an interest in learning. Key, therefore, is understanding what motivates you. Successfully motivating yourself depends on a number of factors, including:

- promoting your own development;

- managing your own experience;

- regulating your emotions;

- regulating your behaviour; and

- accepting oneself.

- Author of *Awaken the Giant Within* and *Unlimited Power*.
- One of the great influencers of his generation.
- Leading thinker in the psychology of personal achievement and peak performance.

It is this latter point that most people find difficult because of the way we were brought up and the way we perceive ourselves. Part of the reason for understanding yourself should be to become more comfortable with what and who you are or, if this is not the case, to act as the catalyst for change.

SMART PEOPLE
TO HAVE ON
YOUR SIDE:

ANTHONY
ROBBINS

Emotional intelligence

The roots of emotional intelligence lie in research at New York University that discovered the significant role of the amygdala in controlling our emotions. The amygdala is part of the brain's emotional system, known as the limbic system, and can be considered to be a database of emotional memories. These memories are crude, pre-programmed responses to external stimuli. For example, if confronted by a tiger, the amygdala would cause the person confronted to run; there would be little value in taking time to weigh up options or to consider the outcomes in more detail. The reason why this is so is because information reaches the amygdala before those parts of the brain that are responsible for reasoning. This means that an emotional response to a situation can override the more rational response derived from the cortex. It is the cortex that processes the much wider set of information necessary to develop a considered response. Emotional intelligence therefore depends on our ability to understand and control the automatic responses created by the amygdala, and reversing the tendency for emotions to override reasoning.

We all should recognize that the rules of work are changing, and our ability to get on is no longer framed by intelligence, training, and expertise alone. It increasingly depends on how well we handle other people and ourselves. Emotional intelligence entered management thinking with the publication of Daniel Goleman's book *Emotional Intelligence,* and his second, *Working with Emotional Intelligence.* He argues that there is a growing recognition that emotional intelligence skills are a vital component of the modern corporation. This is especially true because most organizations are now heavily dependent upon people rather than products, and being successful within the knowledge economy depends upon how well people work together, which extends to how well they relate to each other at the emotional level. There are five elements to being emotionally intelligent (which as you will see, overlaps somewhat with NLP):

- Being self-aware. Essentially, understanding how we tick, including understanding our weaknesses as well as our strengths.

- Managing the effects of our emotions. This means considering how and when to apply our emotions rather than responding automatically. This is very similar to the NLP model (event plus response equals outcome).

- Maintaining our motivation under a variety of circumstances.

- Understanding the emotions of others. This means paying attention to how other people feel and being attuned to the subtle signals displayed by others as you interact with them. This feeds into the second zone of lifelong learning – interpersonal skills.

- Managing relationships. This covers how relationships in their widest sense are managed and maintained. This again falls into zone two.

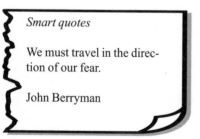

Smart quotes

We must travel in the direction of our fear.

John Berryman

Myers Briggs Type Indicator®[3]

The Myers Briggs Type Indicator® was developed as a way of understanding the differences between the way people behaved and as a way of improving interpersonal communication and teamworking. It also allowed individuals to understand more about themselves, their motivations, and the way they perceived and reacted to the world around them. The basis of our behaviour (and how we act with other people) can be described across four dimensions. First, where our primary source of energy comes from, which will either be from the external environment (extrovert (E)) or from within ourselves (introvert (I)). Second, your preference for taking in information, which will either be in the form of facts (sensing (S)) or patterns and concepts (intuition (N)). Third, the way you make decisions, which will either be based upon the application of logic and facts (thinking (T)) or on the way you sense and feel things around you (feeling (F)). And finally, the way you manage your life, which will either be organized (judgement (J)) or flexible (perception (P)). Taken together, the four dimensions lead to 16 possible personality types, briefly outlined below.

- ESTJ – prefers the outer world rather than the inner, likes to deal in facts, is organized, and likes detail. Tends to be practically-orientated and prefers to apply known methods when dealing with problems and projects.

- INFP – is inward-focused, prefers patterns and concepts, tends to rely on feelings when making decisions, and has a flexible outlook on life. Likes work that has meaning, and likes to work with other people.

- ESFP – is externally facing, deriving energy from the outside world, prefers facts, is both practical and people-orientated, and takes a practical approach to life. Tends to be impulsive and loves to fire-fight.

- INTJ – prefers the internal world of inner thoughts, is strongly intellectual, preferring to deal with strategic and future concepts but is also able to deal with the detail of implementation, and is logical and planning-focused with a keen eye on competence and quality. The INTJ is therefore both critical and judgemental.

- ESFJ – prefers the external world and serving others, is very loyal and has a strong sense of purpose. Very much a people person but only in the sense of maintaining good relationships. Tends to be poor at handling and accepting criticism.

- INTP – strongly intellectual, preferring to solve complex problems rather than following routine activities. The INTP is generally quiet, preferring the inner world of thoughts.

- ENFP – externally- and people-focused, and likes to explore ideas that have a people bias. Generally poor at attending to detail and planning, instead preferring to experiment.

- ISTJ – prefers facts and logic, especially when it comes to decision-making. Tends to prefer working on practical rather than abstract problems. Although facts-based, the ISTJ is sensitive to the way things work around them (a good observer).

- ESTP – prefers action to thinking and therefore enjoys solving problems with a practical dimension to them, as well as troubleshooting in times of crisis.

- INFJ – inwardly focused, but with a strong sense of direction, which is usually self-directed. Generally good at understanding people and what makes them tick, and will often coach people to develop their own skills and capabilities.

- ENFJ – a real people person, deriving most of their benefit from working with other people. Takes a genuine interest in other people's development and will help as much as possible in these circumstances. However, the ENFJ does not like criticism.

- ISTP – likes to acquire new information and knowledge and then apply it practically. Although quiet and detached, preferring the inner world of the mind, they can come up with great ideas.

- ENTJ – generally a control freak, preferring to direct and manage in an impersonal way. Also very intolerant of those who are less than competent, or who fail to set themselves high standards.

- ISFP – likes to deal with individuals rather than groups and is very supportive and sensitive to the needs of others. Does not like conflict.

- ENTP – a creative problem-solver who combines the ability to deal with patterns and concepts and the application of logic. Loves testing out new ideas and overcoming obstacles during their implementation. Generally instigates and leads change.

- ISFJ – is loyal, dependable and conscientious, taking the trouble to understand an individual's sensitivities. Hates conflict.

Myers Briggs is widely used within organizations to help staff develop a better understanding of what makes them tick. Very few, however, take it any further by extending it into team development, where most of its benefit can be derived. If you are interested in assessing your personality type (if you haven't already done so), go to www.personalitypage.com. From a lifelong learning perspective, the Myers Briggs indicator can help us determine the process through which we can learn. The following are rules of thumb, which can be used to help frame your approach when implementing your lifelong learning strategy:[4]

- Es (extrovert) favour discussions, trial and error, and learning that involves movement (such as role-plays).

- Is (introvert) prefer pure study and reflection.

- Ss (sensing) like to follow step-by-step guides and processes.

- Ns (intuition) prefer to understand the abstract and theoretical angle of a concept and hence prefer more creative learning methods such as brainstorming.

- Ts (thinking) love the challenge of learning something difficult and prefer to think in terms of systems and logic.

- Fs (feeling) will tend to focus on those things that they are passionate about and ignore the rest. They are also much more focused on the human aspects of learning and therefore would prefer a group-based approach to study.

- Js (judging) enjoy learning by following set tasks that are well-structured with defined learning objectives. In essence, they need to see a purpose to the learning.

- Ps (perceiving) will immerse themselves in a situation and learn from the environment. They prefer fun and flexibility and, as with the extravert, will enjoy role-playing exercises.

Interpersonal

Leadership

Leadership is a skill that is often quoted as being critical within the workplace. Companies can succeed and fail because of it, and we all look to people who display leadership qualities. The problem for most of us, however, is that leadership is poorly understood and few of us know how to create it. What is clear is that it takes on many different forms, including:[5]

- Dictatorial – usually associated with totalitarian states and includes people such as Hitler, Stalin, and Genghis Khan. There are, of course, plenty of dictators in modern businesses.

- Benevolent – normally a paternal and nurturing form of leadership, with a wider interest in others around them. Examples include the Pope and Mother Theresa.

- Visionary – typically someone who is capable of seeing the future and taking others with them. This would include Martin Luther King, John F. Kennedy, and Margaret Thatcher during her first term in office.

- Collaborative – a rare form of leadership which involves the leader being with his or her people. In other words, to be seen as being part of the team rather than remote. A good example is Richard Branson.

- Hero – heroic leadership, particularly when a country or company is under threat is vital and there are plenty of examples including George Washington, Nelson Mandela, and Winston Churchill.

- Actor – leaders have to be great at performing be it through telling stories, making presentations and speeches, or playing the role of the leader. Examples include Bill Gates, Alfred Sloan, and Percy Barnevik of ABB

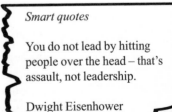

Smart quotes

You do not lead by hitting people over the head – that's assault, not leadership.

Dwight Eisenhower

Whatever form leadership takes, the difficulty we have is trying to define it and emulate it because it is hard to boil it down into a series of dos and don'ts. Despite this problem of definition, we must all be capable of demonstrating leadership qualities both when dealing with our colleagues and when directing our own personal development. In many cases this involves using what Roger Fisher and Alan Sharp term lateral leadership, which is usually associated with getting things done when you do not have the positional or status power to do so. Fisher and Sharp believe there are five elements to getting things done which can be applied irrespective of whether or not you have the legitimized power to do so:[6]

1   Having a sense of purpose. No matter if you are working alone or within a group, if you have no sense of purpose you will not get things done. It is this that drives us to complete things.

2   Taking time to think. Most people's thinking is fragmented and un-structured. By following a more structured approach, people can achieve more. This is especially important in lifelong learning.

3   Learning. Thinking alone will not lead to effective solutions. Therefore, it is important to test out new ideas in the real world, and use the feed-back we receive to enhance our learning.

4   Engagement. In general, the challenges you set yourself and others will frame the response. If these are unexciting, the motivation to complete them will be limited. So, one of the major success factors in both per-sonal and team leadership is creating an exciting environment in which we are committed to completing the task in hand.

5   Feedback. We may not always enjoy receiving feedback, but it is one of the best ways we can learn.

It should be clear that the principles of the seven zones can be applied within lifelong learning as they provide a great navigational tool for framing and directing your learning.

- Author of *Authentic Leadership* and *Seven Zones for Leadership*.
- Divides human action into seven distinct but related components: power, structure, resources, mission, meaning, existence, and fulfilment.
- Links these components to seven zones of leadership:

1. Serving the past – understanding the past is an essential component of effective leadership in the future.
2. Building core competencies – this is about spotting and developing the skills required to deliver an organization's products and services.
3. Systems thinking – this focuses on the infrastructure required to connect the competences in zone two and creating a shared identity and purpose.
4. Creating ownership – this is associated with empowering those around you to make things happen.
5. Focusing on the future – this combines setting the strategic direction and managing the change as people move from the present and into the unknown future.
6. Creating meaning in chaos – in essence, leading in times of uncertainty.
7. Serving the promise of authenticity – living the vision and leading by example.

SMART PEOPLE
TO HAVE ON
YOUR SIDE:

ROBERT TERRY

Teamwork

In the modern business, the majority of things are achieved through teams. The importance of working in teams is growing as we depend more on our ability to manage and exploit our knowledge. Understanding the dynamics of teams and how they develop is an essential part of your interpersonal

Smart quotes

Whoever you are, business executive, union member, staff support, consultant or government official, you cannot accomplish your goals yourself. You need subordinates, coworkers, superiors, suppliers or customers – people you depend on every day. Unless you are a hermit, there is no way you can get much done alone. So you work with others.

Roger Fisher and Alan Sharp

development. Indeed, many organizations now seek 360 degree feedback that often extends to teamworking and team-building skills and, where these are found lacking, the person concerned will find it hard to succeed within the organization.

Great teams have a number of characteristics. First, they tend to have a very clear mission about what they are going to achieve. So, whether this is a project team implementing a new IT system, or a research and development team attempting to develop a new product, a clear mission is essential to success. Second, every team member understands the interdependencies between them and everyone else in the team; in essence, knowing what is expected from everyone and how one person in the team depends on another. This is, of course, essential as otherwise the team would become dysfunctional and their efforts would fail. Third, they are cohesive. Sharing a common goal, and understanding what each person wants to achieve personally out of the experience (what's in it for me), ensures the team maintains its solidarity. The final component is trust. Ultimately, teams work well when each member trusts all others. Trust is the kingpin of any team and without it, the team will never perform to its highest potential.

Great teams are not, however, created overnight as they usually have to pass through five stages of development of which the first two are critical to the creation of a functional and effective team:

1   Forming. This is where the team get together for the first time. They don't know each other and the team at this stage can be considered to be a collection of individuals without any knowledge of their fellow team members. Forming is therefore all about getting to know the dynamics of the team as they begin to develop the cohesiveness required to be high performing.

SMART VOICES

THE GULF WAR COALITION

The sheer effort required by the Gulf War coalition during Operation Desert Storm is testament to the benefits of teamwork and the following quote sums it up:

'Thus began one of the most innovative, seat-of-the-pants operations ever undertaken. As more and more units were deployed in theater, the scientist, computer nerds and whiz kids had to patch together a voice and data network using whatever came to hand, while in the United States their support services scrambled to pull together and ship out the hardware they needed. In the end, over 200 sorties by C-141 Starfighter transport aircraft were required to carry the equipment to the Gulf, in the process virtually draining the USAF of tactical and strategic communications equipment. In the end, the communications effort involved 2300 personnel, 12 combat communications squadrons, 7000 radio frequencies, 1000 miles of land links, 59 communications centers, over 29 million calls, all in support of the 350,000 air operations in Desert Shield and the 225,000 in Desert Storm. It is testament to the skill and imagination of the technicians involved that the system worked, because nothing on that size or scale had ever been envisioned, let alone created.'[7]

2   Storming. As the team gets to know each other and more about their purpose, rivalries, friction, and conflict emerge. This is perfectly natural as members within the team need to find their place within the team and work out who is to do what. Trying to suppress the storming behaviour is usually counter-productive in the long term because it forces conflict underground and can damage team performance later on.

3   Norming. This is where the team begins to gel and the behaviours of each individual conforms to the unwritten rules of the team (in essence its culture). It is at this stage that the team becomes more important than the individual. Moreover, people begin to develop mutual respect for each other and begin to provide mutual support.

4 Performing. This is where the team becomes high-performing.

5 Adjourning. Once the task is complete, the team will be disbanded and its members will go their separate ways. Ironically this can be the most difficult period for any team, especially if they have been together for a long period of time. In such cases, emotions similar to bereavement can be experienced, which can often require careful management.

Teamworking is particularly important within lifelong learning because:

- It provides a great opportunity to learn from other people when working on a similar task.

- It allows you develop the interpersonal skills you need within the workplace.

- It exposes you to the full gamut of human behaviour, thereby allowing you to develop coping strategies required to deal with difficult people.

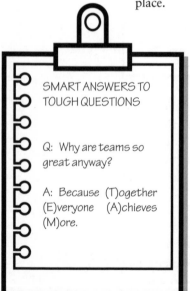

SMART ANSWERS TO
TOUGH QUESTIONS

Q: Why are teams so great anyway?

A: Because (T)ogether (E)veryone (A)chieves (M)ore.

Organizational politics

Politics should be expected in any organization, and dealing with its various forms is a core skill for anyone who wishes to progress. Many people complain about the political nature of their workplace and shy away from it because they perceive it to be associated with manipulation, sucking-up, bullying, blaming, and so on. However, it is essential that we all take the trouble to understand the politics of our organizational environment and be prepared to embrace and apply it.

There are three underlying reasons why politics exists within organizations:[8]

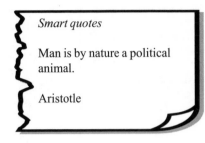

Smart quotes

Man is by nature a political animal.

Aristotle

1   Competition for scarce or prized resources. This includes physical resources such as equipment and office space, as well as human capital, position, and status. It is not uncommon to see political problems arise within projects that require the same skilled resources as the operational line, nor is it surprising to see arguments and backstabbing associated with roles, responsibilities, and positions within organizations. In both circumstances, there would be no politics if resources were in abundant supply, or there was no real competition for positions of power.

2   Self-interest. Although there are many people within organizations who place organizational interests above their own, there are a significant minority who will pursue a path of self-interest. This may mean that they appear to do the right thing for the organization, but it is usually masking ulterior motives.

3   Power and the struggle to achieve it. The feeling of having no power is unbearable for the majority of people and when anything is altering the balance of power, a political reaction should be expected. Interestingly, nothing has really changed since the times of the mediaeval court. Here, the courtiers had to be elegant, committed, and friendly, whilst scheming and plotting in the background. Overt power plays were frowned upon and could end in imprisonment or death. Today the same rules apply; people must appear civilized, decent, democratic, and fair, but none of us can take these rules too literally, as we will be crushed by those who are plotting around us.

SMART VOICES

MANAGEMENT CONSULTANT

Whilst working in a government department, a senior manager was proving to be a major blocker in a major organizational change. Although the person concerned was smart and technically valuable to the department, he was unwilling to change his behaviours. So, rather than tackling this head-on, a political solution was created with his director. The real skill in making this happen was keeping the political manoeuvring behind the scenes so that the senior manager was unaware of what was happening. Over a couple of months, the senior manager was initially insulated and then isolated from the change. Then, when his influence on the change process was sufficiently reduced, he was transferred to another department.

In order to manage politics, it is first necessary to identify and analyze them. This can be achieved using the following four steps:[9]

1   Identify the activities and actions that are associated with the organization's scarce and prized resources. Political infighting typically occurs around such things as change projects, technology investments, research and development, and product development. Increasingly, the reduction in the number of senior management positions within organizations has led to much higher stakes between those who seek the trappings of power. As a result, there is significantly more political infighting between those who wish to become the senior managers of the future. Once the sources of political battles have been identified, it is necessary to identify everyone who is involved, as this will help to frame the extent of the political landscape that has to be managed.

2   Identify the motivations behind competitive activities. Successfully managing politics requires the identification of the motivations of those involved. Therefore, the creation of a stakeholder map that identifies the key relationships, rivalries, and alliances can be very useful to assess how people relate to each other in an organization.

- Professor of organization development and psychology at Loyala University of Chicago.
- Author of *Working the Shadow Side*.
- Shows how to use behind the scenes management to get things done.
- Describes how we can practice politics.

SMART PEOPLE
TO HAVE ON
YOUR SIDE:

GERARD EGAN

3   Identify the sources of power. Power resides in five fundamental forms: positional power, which is the legitimized power that exists in a person's position within an organization; status power, which exists by virtue of the title people are given, even when they have no real positional power (for example, non-executive directors); resource power resides in anyone who manages or owns scarce resource – such people have probably the strongest source of power – that associated with veto – and, although they may be quite low within the organization's hierarchy, they can wield significant power over the success of any initiative. The final source of power is that associated with expertise. The guru or subject-matter expert can be a powerful figure in any organization.

4   Assess the political strategies adopted by those who seek power or control over scarce resources. For completeness, I have included some of the common political strategies used within organizations (see Table 5.1). It should be remembered, of course, that these political behaviours are essentially about the acquisition or retention of power and little else.[10]

Q: Why should I take the trouble to understand office politics?

A: Politics is part of the fabric of any organization, and learning how to use it will help you achieve what you want in your career.

Smart
answers to
tough
questions

Table 5.1 Common political behaviours.

Political behaviour	Description
Ownership	An individual or group owns a project, product line, department, process and benefits from the status and rights of ownership. Ownership is all about control by being there first. Within projects, it is the ownership of resources that typically creates the greatest amount of political turbulence.
Information manipulation	Knowledge is power. More information generates more filters through which information must pass, and each filter provides ample opportunity for information distortion. Typical tactics include withholding information, and manipulating it to change the message (for example, distorting bad news to appear good, or not divulging it). Information manipulation is increasingly linked to ownership.
Alliances	Political battles within organizations usually involve taking sides. Types of behaviour include those associated with sycophants, sleepers (waiting to join the winning side), shoulder rubbers (face-to-face contacts), and those that monopolize others' time.
Invisible walls	This is especially applicable to projects where rules, procedures, and information access are placed in the path of a project to slow it down, derail it, and generally prevent it from achieving its objectives. The invisible wall game is best played by those who can maintain the appearance of sincere effort, but without actually achieving anything.
Strategic non-compliance	Agreeing upfront to co-operate, and then defaulting on the agreement at the last minute, leaving little or no opportunity for the other party to do anything about it.
Discrediting	It is said that reputation is one of the cornerstones of power, and once lost is almost impossible to regain. Therefore, discrediting individuals is one of the surest ways to gain power.
Camouflage	The purpose of camouflage is to distract or confuse people long enough to defuse or deflect a course of action. Camouflage can sometimes be associated with discrediting.

Technical

What falls into the technical dimension of lifelong learning is entirely driven by the function you work in now, and the one in which you may desire to work in the future (which you will have a view on when you create your lifelong learning strategy in the next chapter). So, if you are working within finance for example, you will probably focus on the technical needs of a financial role, whilst if you are in marketing, you will focus on developing technical skills in communication and creativity.

There is little value in covering every single organizational discipline within this section because there is so much knowledge required to master any one of the myriad specialisms that exist within a business. Moreover, you will know best when it comes to your immediate technical learning needs. There are two exceptions I would make. The first is with information technology, which is so critical to the modern business that it cannot and should not be ignored. And the second is project management, which is a core skill for the lifelong learner.

Information Technology (IT)

IT is driving much of the change around us and we would be wise to gain a general understanding of its major components and of its implications on us and our working environments. This is as important for those who work in technology as for those who consider themselves to be purely business-focused. Because of the centrality of IT to any business, being comfortable with its application and understanding its importance in the business is now a necessary skill.

In order to remain IT-savvy, it is necessary to have knowledge of the following:

- IT's basic architectural components. Many people are confused by IT because they lack even a basic understanding of how it is pieced together. And although some of the deeply technical aspects of IT change continuously, its general architecture remains fairly constant. All IT can be viewed as being built up from a number of layers:[11]

SMART PEOPLE
TO HAVE ON
YOUR SIDE:

CHARLES
WANG

- Chairman and CEO of Computer Associates.
- Author of *Technovision*.
- Believes that the fundamental problem that organizations have with IT is due to the business and IT communities failing to communicate.

- Hardware – the physical component of IT which includes servers, network routers, personal computers and peripherals such as printers.
- Operating systems – the software that controls the basic functions and operations of the hardware.
- Databases – where the essential data and information of the business are held.
- Middleware – typically the interface between the underlying data held in the databases and the applications used by the business. Sometimes they might be intermediate applications that translate the data from one application to another as it moves around the organization.
- Applications – the business and technical systems that manipulate data and information to add business value.
- User interfaces – where the user accesses the information and functionality they need to perform their daily activities.

- IT trends. Keeping abreast of what is changing, or predicted to change within IT, is a necessity. Where you monitor such trends, very much depends upon where you sit in relation to the panoply of IT. If you are at executive level, then being aware of what new technologies mean for the business is much more important than knowing what they mean in terms of how they are constructed and deployed. If you are working at the coalface of IT, then the technical detail is far more important, but you must not lose sight of the bigger picture and the business reasons for IT. There are a vast number of magazines, journals, electronic subscription services, and organizations such as Gartner and Forrester, that can help you keep up to date, and there are also those that take a peek into the future. The key thing is to tap into these as much as you need to.

- Impacts of IT. We have already seen in earlier chapters that IT can profoundly change the way we work. Here are some examples:
  - IT will affect the way the organization is structured and how work is executed. For example, ten years ago we would not have been able to work remotely or globally that easily.
  - Customer management. We are now able to capture and manipulate vast amounts of information about our customers so that we can target them and service their needs more effectively.
  - Product development. Manufacturing technologies have speeded up dramatically so that it is now possible to manufacture customized goods on demand. Mass production is out, and mass customization is in.

- The pitfalls of IT. We should be under no illusion that IT is not without its problems. There are major issues with how the business and IT communities communicate and work together, leading to poor IT systems and major project failures. Setting realistic expectations, understanding how IT can add value, and capturing the essential requirements are some of the ways in which IT can add value, as opposed to destroying it.

Project management

The importance of project management has grown considerably over the last 30 years. Originating in the aerospace industry during the 1950s when

WAL-MART

Wal-Mart have transformed the way they manage their stock using sophisticated IT systems and networks. By capturing detailed point of sale information at each of their stores, combining it and sending it back to suppliers, Wal-Mart have increased the efficiency in inventory management, ordering and shipping. Suppliers no longer have to send reps, instead receiving information direct from Wal-Mart about what products are needed – and where – on a daily basis.

SMART VOICES

constructing large passenger planes was a major departure from traditional aircraft manufacture, project management has become an important discipline within most businesses. Getting to grips with the basic skills of project management is useful as it is likely that you will be involved with projects at some stage in your career, even if you are not leading them. And, if you have a desire to become a project manager, then it is very important to augment your basic understanding with training and experience. Below are what I believe to be the core skills of a project manager:

- A focus on planning. This means investing sufficient time in planning the project, and not leaping straight into the scheduling tool (such as Microsoft Project). Planning is more than just creating a Gantt chart – it involves determining what the project is to achieve, what it is going to produce, what techniques and tools it is to apply, and what resources it requires to achieve these. This is not an overnight process, and nor is it something that the project manager should do in isolation. Engaging the project team and wider stakeholder community during the planning process can provide many benefits.

- A focus on monitoring, control, and visibility. Once started, the project has to be monitored and controlled. Monitoring and controlling typically involves the management of the plan, the resources, and the constraints under which the project is executed – usually time and money, and occasionally quality. Ensuring this is visible to the project stakeholders is very important. Visibility, however, is not about distributing the Gantt chart. In general, the Gantt is only designed to serve the project manager and their immediate team, as it allows the tasks and their duration to be tracked. Visibility is about ensuring that the mechanism, be it primarily graphical or data based, allows the project's status and prognosis to be clearly understood by all project stakeholders.

- A focus on communication. Communication is the lifeblood of any project. It has to be continuous and depends to a great extent on the project manager. Uncommunicative project managers, who are unwilling to talk to their team or their project stakeholders, are a significant danger to any project.

- A focus on benefits. Benefits realization should be the only reason why projects are initiated. Too many projects fail to deliver any significant benefits and, even when they do, these are usually way below those that were anticipated at the time of the business case. Being able to report on the status of the project from a benefits perspective is a valuable addition to project reporting, and demonstrates to senior management that the project manager is concerned about the outcomes of the project, and not just the project itself.

- A sensitivity for power and politics. Many project managers shy away from power and politics because they believe it is difficult to manage, or feel that it is unimportant – as long as they deliver the project, everything will be fine. There is plenty of evidence to suggest the opposite is true, as major projects involve a varying degree of power and politics. Being attuned to this, and managing it in a sensitive way allows the project manager to steer the project through the often turbulent political waters.

Environmental

The environmental dimension to lifelong learning should concentrate on understanding the wider context of our working and non-working lives. Changes in economic circumstances affects us all, either through redundancy, mergers, acquisitions, or overseas assignments, so it is increasingly difficult to remain ignorant of them. Ignorance often leads to nasty surprises. Part of the skill of lifelong learning is having sufficient knowledge of the wider economic and business environments so that it is possible to navigate our way through the uncertainties that the future holds. Learning to recognize the trends around us and the patterns of change means that the future and our careers will be less scary and a little more certain. There are two other elements to the wider environmental learning that we need. The first is to gain a better understanding of international cultures so that when we inevitably work with people from other nationalities, we have a better understanding of how to make the relationship work successfully. The second is risk management. Future-proofing our careers and maintaining our employability in the face of an uncertain future requires an astute management of risk. Therefore, getting to grips with its core principles is essential.

Business and economics

As we progress in our careers, we need to develop a better understanding of the business environment, which extends into the general and global economies. This does not mean that you have to become an expert economist, for example, but it does mean that you have to develop a basic knowledge of how economics works. The popularity of MBAs reflects this need to develop and it would be a good idea to look at a typical MBA curriculum and use this to direct your learning. Typical subject areas would include:

- general management;

- finance and accounting;

- human resource management;

- macroeconomics and microeconomics;

- marketing and sales;

- strategic management and direction setting; and

- organizational design.

You can keep abreast of the general business environment by reading quality newspapers, journals, and magazines. If you augment this with targeted learning, you will soon develop a good understanding of what is going on around you.

Intercultural working

As we have seen, for those of us with skills and knowledge that are in demand, it is possible to work without frontiers. And for those working in multinational and transnational corporations, tours of duty overseas are often part of the process of becoming a global citizen and a necessary step for moving up the hierarchy. However, Terrence Deal and Allan Kennedy, authors of *The New Corporate Cultures*, believe that the global economy has caused severe strains on corporate cultures. They believe that rapid globalization has caught people unprepared for conducting cross-cultural business transactions and has resulted in the tendency to stereotype. Therefore, to succeed in a global workplace, we must embrace another aspect of our lifelong learning: understanding national cultures. Thankfully, some of the most enlightening and useful research on national culture is available to us all. Geert Hofstede, who studied 116,000 IBM employees around the world (who were identical in terms of position and role and only differed in respect of their nationality), identified four dimensions of national culture:[12]

- The power distance. Hofstede defined this as the extent to which the less powerful members of institutions and organizations within a country expect and accept that power is distributed unequally. In practice, this means the degree to which subordinates are willing to question their superiors and push back against decisions. Such pushback is more prevalent in western societies and less common in the Far East. Furthermore, where the acceptance of inequality is greatest, paternalistic and auto-cratic management styles tend to dominate, whilst the opposite is true in those countries where inequality is less acceptable. Here, management tends to be more consultative. This is typical of the Low Countries, such as the Netherlands.

- Individualism–collectivism. This refers to the extent to which people within a society are expected to fend for themselves and their immediate families. The more one is expected to fend for oneself, the more individualistic the society. The opposite of this is collectivism, where from birth, people are integrated into strong, cohesive groups which tend to be maintained throughout life. As is to be expected, in those societies that are more collective, decision-making tends to be group-based, and as a consequence often slower (for example, the Nordic countries) than in those countries that are more individualistic (for example, the United States and the United Kingdom).

- Masculinity–femininity. In those societies that can be considered masculine, emphasis tends to be placed on achievement, ambition, and success (for example, the United States), whilst in those countries that are more feminine, the emphasis is on quality of work and caring for others (for example, Finland, Holland, and Sweden). As expected, in those countries that are more masculine, working hours tend to be longer (for example, the United Kingdom and the United States), whilst in those that are more feminine, work is a means to an end, not the end itself (for example, the Netherlands).

- Uncertainty avoidance. This refers to the extent to which members of a culture feel threatened by uncertain or unknown circumstances. In those countries where uncertainty avoidance is high, people attempt to reduce it through structure, process, and familiarity so that events are clearly interpretable. This is true of Germany, Switzerland, and France.

ABB

SMART VOICES

Since its creation through the merger of ASEA of Sweden and Brown Boveri and Company of Switzerland, it has achieved an amazing degree of convergence and consistency across a wide range of countries and cultures. Although it has acquired and merged with many companies from around the world, it has preserved and promoted the national cultures of each. But as well as preserving the local cultures, ABB has developed a global culture that ensures it does not fracture into national islands. So, although factories are spread around the world, they all form part of global groups that share technology and best practice. Cross border co-operation is also enhanced through the use of multicultural teams. Few of ABB's 5000 profit centres are viable as stand-alone entities – they depend on each other for ideas, information, and resources. This engenders a sprit of learning, connectivity, and collaboration, vital to the success of the global firm.

In addition, where uncertainty avoidance is high, people are less likely to question superiors and tend to avoid situations that involve conflict. In those countries that have a weak uncertainty avoidance, there tends to be less concern or need for strict rules; people are generally more self-governing, conflict is seen as non-threatening and an important part of the workplace. Furthermore, individuals are generally more flexible. This is typical of the United States, United Kingdom, and Australia.

The work of Mark Williams[13] can also help us understand some of the attitudes and behaviours we have in relation to working overseas and multicultural teams He identified ten lenses of culture which affect the way people perceive others from different nationalities. The lenses can help you understand the way you see variations in such things as race, culture, and ethnicity and can be used to generate an additional level of sensitivity beyond that established by Hofstede. The ten lenses are:

1 Assimilationist. Those who want people to submerge their individual and cultural identities in favour of nationalistic and patriotic ideals.

2 Colourblind. Those who see people as individuals and ignore race, colour, ethnicity, and other external cultural factors.

3 Culturalcentrist. Those who seek to improve the welfare of their cultural group by accentuating their history and identity.

4 Elitist. Those who believe in the superiority of the upper class and embrace the importance of family roots, wealth, and social status.

5 Integrationist Those who support the breaking down of all barriers between racial groups by merging people of different cultures together in communities and in the workplace.

6 Meritocratist. The individualist credo: if you have the abilities and work hard enough, you can compete with anyone to make your dreams come true.

7 Multiculturalist. Those who celebrate the diversity of cultures and the contributions they make to national culture and history.

8 Seclusionist. Those who feel strongly that they should protect themselves from racial, cultural, and/or ethnic groups that diminish the character and quality of their group's experiences within society.

9 Transcendent. Those who focus on the human spirit, people's universal connection, and shared humanity.

10 Victim/caretaker. Those who feel that they are still suffering from the generational impact of previous oppression and therefore deserve compensation from society and the dominant culture.

Risk management

We live in uncertain times. Competitive markets, globalization, booms, busts, recessions, technological change, war, climatic change, and so on: all present risks to a varying degree. In many respects, we are all used to dealing with a certain level of risk within our daily lives. After all, walking across the road has an inherent risk associated with it. But unless we are doing something that departs significantly from our daily routine, such as jumping out of a plane for example, we tend to take risk for granted and we often don't give it a second's thought. Also, at the individual level, if we take a risk and fail to manage it properly, the damage is limited to us, and maybe our near relatives. The management of risk for organizations is not as simple for two reasons. First, because the implications of poor risk management can have significant impacts for a wider number of stakeholders including shareholders, employees, and the national and local economies. And second, because the nature of risk within organizations is far more complex than the simple risks we have to manage as individuals. Managing risk is an essential skill of all modern corporations. Risk falls into five broad categories:

Smart quotes

There is nothing wrong with risk. It is the lifeblood of business and the test of entrepreneurs and managers. What matters is how you handle risk and the culture in which you operate.

John Holliwell

- Strategic risk. This is associated with those risks that can affect the strategic direction and survival of the organization. Factors that play into this category include the macroeconomic risks created by the fiscal policies of central and federal governments, as well as the impacts of disruptive technologies, such as the Internet. Such risks are also associated with poor business decisions and direction setting, and extend to such things as mergers and acquisitions. It is well known, for example, that 80 per cent of mergers and acquisitions never realize the benefits expected of them. Considering the amount of money invested in such ventures, the very fact that so many fail suggests poor risk management.

- Business/financial risk. This covers those risks that can affect the business in terms of its general financial viability. It includes risks associated with the market in which the organization operates (market risk), as well as the ability to finance growth through loans (credit risk). These risks are generally well understood, with a large number of financial instruments and techniques available to the risk manager.

- Programme and project risk. This is the risk that a major change initiative could fail or the benefits expected of it do not materialize. With an increasing use of projects and programmes to drive through change within organizations, this type of risk is often closely associated with strategic risk, as failure can have significant impacts on the organization. Moreover, with the increasing complexity of organizations, managing this type of risk is fast becoming an essential skill.

- Operational risk. This is a wide-ranging category of risk that includes the failure of any aspect of a business' operations. This includes management failure, system and software failure, human error, process inefficiencies, and procedural failures. Although comparatively new, it is recognized as being an important part of an overall risk management framework.

- Technological risk. This is different from operational risk in that it is associated with bringing new technology products to market and introducing new technology (and IT systems) into the organizational setting, both of which are high-risk ventures.

The basic form of risk management involves four continuous stages:

- Identification. This involves the organization identifying the types of risk they might be exposed to. Some are more obvious and manageable than others. The key point is to identify those risks that can be managed. Identifying risks that are way outside of your control means that little can be done to manage them, resulting in time and effort being spent to no avail. In such instances, it would be better to develop contingency and business continuity plans to address the risk once it has materialized.

- Quantification. This involves assessing the severity of the risk which, in its simplest form, is the product of its impact (which is usually assessed in terms of financial loss), and the probability or likelihood of occurrence. Because it can be very difficult to make precise assessments of probability and impact, most organizations rate each dimension using high, medium, and low, where each represents a range rather than a precise figure. This makes it easier to rank the risks when it comes to choosing those it intends to manage.

- Managing or responding. This requires the organization to establish a course of action that will address the risk. Organizations have five responses. First, they can transfer the risk by passing it to a third party. For example, one of the reasons why so many organizations have outsourced their information technology is to pass the technological risk to those who are better positioned to manage it. Second, they can avoid the risk by taking a different course of action, and third, they can reduce the risk by taking action that minimizes its impact or probability. Fourth, they can put some contingency in place that allows the organization to cope with the implications of the risk should it materialize. This was an essential component to preparing for Year 2000, for example. Finally, they can accept the risk and its consequences. Ultimately, before this strategy is adopted it is important to understand the impacts of the risk and how much it would cost the organization in terms of money and resources to manage it. Balancing the two will allow an appropriate decision to be made.

- Monitoring and controlling. Risks are time-based events and as such, their impact and probability will vary with time. This is well known within banking, but less so in the other areas of risk, such as strategic and operational risk. Monitoring risk has two strands to it. The first is to ensure that the actions agreed during the response stage are undertaken and that their effect on the risk's impact and probability is tracked. And the second is to monitor the risk over time, as other events will cause the risk's probability and impact to increase or decrease.

Part of the skill of managing your career involves managing risk. As we saw in Chapter 3, you need to be able to future-proof your career, and part of this involves managing the risks associated with following a specialist or generalist career path. Moreover, if you aspire to a senior management position, it is a key skill you will need.

This chapter has skimmed across a number of key areas that should be core to any lifelong strategy. I believe that if you have gained even a basic understanding of each of these areas you will begin to connect the concepts associated with each together. And it is this ability to connect that will improve your learning capabilities and also make you a valuable commodity in your organization. Naturally, there is a vast amount of material to cover, but in order to make it manageable it is very important to direct your learning carefully. This is really the purpose of the next chapter, which is all about creating your lifelong learning strategy. Once you have created this, you will know which areas should be tackled and when. The how of lifelong learning comes in Chapter 7.

Notes

1 Gallwey, T. (2000) *The Inner Game of Work*. New York: Texere.

2 Kohn, A. (1993) *Punished by Rewards: The Trouble With Gold Stars, Incentive Plans, A's, Praise and Other Bribes*. New York: Houghton Mifflin, p. 270.

3 For an excellent introduction of Myers Briggs see: Myers, S. (1995) *Influencing People Using Myers Briggs*, Wirral: Team Technology. The summary descriptions of the 16 types is derived from pp. 14–18.

4 See Bayne, R. (1997) *The Myers Briggs Type Indicator®*. Cheltenham: Stanley Thornes (publishers) Ltd. p. 125.

5 See Terry, R. (2001) *Seven Zones for Leadership: Acting Authentically in Stability and Chaos*. California: Davies-Black Publishing, pp. 55–56, and Brown, A. (1999) *The Six Dimensions of Leadership*. London: Random House Business Books.

6 Fisher, R. & Sharp, A. (1999) *Lateral Leadership: Getting Things Done When You Are Not the Boss*. London: HarperCollins Business, pp. 9–10.

7 Adams, J. (1999) *The Next World War: The Warriors and Weapons of the New Battlefields in Cyberspace*. London: Arrow Books, pp. 35–36.

8 Egan, G. (1994) *Working the Shadow Side: A Guide to Positive Behind-the-scenes Management*. San Francisco: Jossey-Bass, p. 196.

9 *Ibid*, pp. 197–211.

10 This table has been derived from Simmons, A. (1998) *Territorial Games: Understanding and Ending Turf Wars at Work*. New York: Amacom.

11 Cox, J. (1999) *Executive's Guide to Information Technology*. New York: John Wiley & Sons, p. 24.

12 Hofstede, G. (1994) *Cultures and Organization: Intercultural Cooperation and its Importance for Survival*. London: HarperCollins Business.

13 Williams, M. (2001) *The 10 Lenses: Your Guide to Living and Working in a Multicultural World*. Capital Books.

6

Developing Your Lifelong Learning Strategy

Now that we have introduced some of the areas that you ought to consider covering within your lifelong strategy, we can now describe how you can develop it. There is no beating about the bush with this, as it is all about ensuring you have an interesting and stimulating career working for an employer (or clients) that you find great to work with. Ironically, very few of us pay enough attention to our career, which usually means it becomes a succession of haphazard choices which we don't tend to enjoy very much. Just ask yourself how much fun you are having at work and within your career; be brutally honest, as there is no point in deluding yourself. I believe that the overriding reasons for developing and following your lifelong learning strategy is to create a real sense of purpose and enjoyment in your work. Better this than going through the motions like the majority seem to do.

Smart quotes

People working in unsatisfactory jobs with poor opportunities are often unhappier than those who have no job at all. A general air of unhappiness is stifling creativity at work: there is too much insecurity, pressure and unconstructive criticism.

Roger Elgin

Smart things
to say about
lifelong learning

Your organization owes you nothing, so if you don't take control, then you have no one else to blame but yourself.

One of the best ways to develop your strategy for lifelong learning is to follow the GROW model. This model is designed to draw out what you want to achieve and how you are going to achieve it by stepping through four stages:

1   Stage 1 is about defining your goals, both in relation to your career, and in terms of what you need to learn.

2   Stage 2 is focused on understanding what is happening now in relation to these goals by assessing what you currently know and what you need to know.

3   Stage 3 helps to explore the variety of options you could take to implement your lifelong learning strategy.

4   Stage 4 is about taking action. In other words, making it happen.

This model recognizes that we all have the resources we need to pursue our goals, if only we knew what they were. This chapter will be structured using the GROW model so that you can walk through the steps required to create your strategy. This is not rocket science, but it does require the necessary commitment to complete it and, most importantly, implement it. There is no room for shelfware.

Stage 1 – identify your goals (the G of the GROW model)

We all have goals in life. Some are well articulated, whilst others appear fanciful. Many are hidden from view, not just from our employers, but from ourselves too. The important thing about goals is to make them explicit by writing them down. The very process of committing them to paper will create an association in your brain and hence make them more likely to occur. However, setting goals without establishing a course of action to meet them will, in the main, ensure that they remain on paper. One of the most important steps to take within lifelong learning is to understand what you need to learn and create your lifelong learning strategy accordingly. But before you can do this, the first step is to understand what your career goals are over the next two to three years and then use these to frame your learning requirements. This stage is designed to answer the following questions:

- Where do you see yourself three years from now?

- How will you know when you have achieved it?

- What will you see, hear, and feel, having achieved your goal?

- What will you know when you have reached this goal?

- How much personal control do you have over your goal?

- What resources do you need to accomplish this goal?

These questions will help you visualize the completion of the goal and help you make it appear real rather than abstract. They will also help you to assess how you will get there and what kind of support from those around you (including your employer) you will need to succeed.

Smart quotes

Individuals who go through the learning paradox over and over again develop greater comfort with ambiguity and uncertainty. They no longer fear the unknown. They develop faith in their abilities to learn.

Jim Harris

Smart quotes

Our aim should be a society in which knowledge, and the power to act on it, are widely spread: distributed intelligence rather than centralized intelligence.

Charles Leadbeater

In answering these questions, you might want to consider what sort of career you wish to have and whether work and achievement are more important than having a full life that is not dominated by work. It is also necessary to determine whether you want to follow a generalist or specialist career. Whatever your choice, it is necessary to know what your medium-term goals are, as otherwise it is likely that you will drift from one job to another without gaining as much as you can from the experiences. And you may end up with skills, attitudes, and behaviours that no one wants five years from now. Example goals might be:

- To have set up a business and be turning over £5 million per annum.

- To have become an expert in project management.

- To have reached a senior management position with my current employer.

The next step during this stage is to consider what sort of things you would like and need to learn. The career goals you established will help you assess where you need to tailor your learning and it is a good idea to group these by the four categories described in the previous chapter.

SMART PEOPLE
TO HAVE ON
YOUR SIDE:

EDDY KNASEL,
JOHN MEED
AND
ANNA
ROSSETTI

- Partners in Learners First, a consultancy at the leading edge of national developments in work-related learning.
- Authors of *Learn For Your Life.*
- Provided a blueprint for continuous learning.
- Believe that the 'three Es' (economy, empowerment, and enjoyment) have replaced the 'three Rs' (reading, writing, and arithmetic).

The other consideration as you develop your goals should be to assess who can help you achieve them; after all, you are not an island. In other words, it is necessary to consider the needs of those who currently employ you (or will in the future). According to Stephen Stumpf and Joel DeLuca, this is the sweet spot,[1] which brings together:

- what you want to do;

- what your employer wants to do; and

- what you can actually do.

This will help to ensure that your strategy is congruent with your employer's. If you don't know what your employer's strategy is, you ought to ask. If you find that your goals are incongruent with your employer's, it will help you to decide where you need to take your career. As I have said throughout this book, in today's workplace you need to be in control and if you are not getting what you need out of your career, you need to take action; the employer won't.

Stage 2 – understand reality and what needs to change (the R of the GROW model)

Having established your lifelong learning goals, which link directly to your career goals, it is necessary to establish where you currently sit in relation to them. In essence, it is about carrying out a knowledge and learning stock-take. The purpose of the reality stage of the GROW model is to answer the following questions:

- What do you know at the moment (in the widest sense)?

- What is missing from this?

- What skills and knowledge do you need to develop (based upon the goals you have set yourself)?

- What skills and knowledge do you need to drop?

- What skills and knowledge do you have which you are not currently using, and hence which you can refresh and exploit?

This stage consists of four steps:

1   Current state assessment which involves understanding what skills you currently have.

2   Blind spot analysis which entails taking a hard look at the gaps in your knowledge.

3   Future profile assessment, which requires you to identify your future skill needs.

4   Skill categorization, which requires you to assess those skills and knowledge that will yield you the most value.

Current state assessment

This first step is very important as it creates the baseline from which you can then assess your blind spots and develop your future profile. Understanding reality should start by assessing your skill/knowledge levels (low, high, or somewhere in between) across the areas you are interested in and then mapping the results onto a simple model such as that of Fig. 6.1. As a starting position you could consider your ability in the following areas:

- team working;

- analytical thinking;

- leadership;

- self development;

- people management;

- project management;

- strategy;

- information technology;

- coaching and mentoring;

- business development;

- negotiation;

- perseverance; and

- risk management.

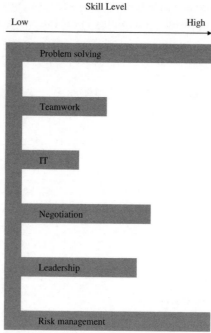

Fig. 6.1   Current state profile.

Blind spot analysis

Once complete, the next thing to do is to assess your knowledge on a wider basis and use this to help identify your most significant blind spots. This can be done using the knowledge grid of Fig. 6.2, which has been updated for lifelong learning. The grid is very simple and is based upon understanding what you know and what you don't know.

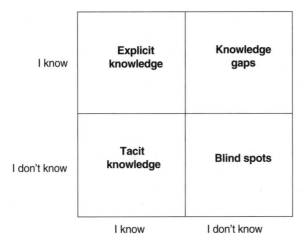

	I know	I don't know
I know	**Explicit knowledge**	**Knowledge gaps**
I don't know	**Tacit knowledge**	**Blind spots**

Fig. 6.2 The knowledge grid.

The grid's four quadrants are:

- Explicit knowledge. These are the things that you know that you know. You can discuss them in detail and you are comfortable in their application. It is easy for you to write these down and explain them to other people. In essence, they are at the forefront of your mind. These are probably the things you are known for in your work and are likely to be functional in nature. This knowledge is well and truly in your comfort zone.

KILLER QUESTIONS

If you had 5 minutes to highlight your key skills and capabilities, could you?

- Tacit knowledge. Here you don't know that you know something. Very often, you will perform tasks or apply knowledge automatically (remember the unconscious competence stage of the four stages of learning?). Sometimes, such knowledge can be lost and, if rarely applied, can disappear from use. This, of course, may allude to the fact that the knowledge is no longer relevant, but it is still worth checking it out before you finally discard it. This knowledge can be very difficult for you to explain to someone else because it requires you to make it explicit again, which itself will help you to test its value. When doing this, it is a good idea to use the four stages of learning in reverse, as discussed in Chapter 4.

- Knowledge gaps. You may already know where the gaps in your knowledge lie and, indeed, be actively trying to plug them. Some will be obvious, such as the functional skills you need to acquire and develop in order to progress in your career. Others may emerge from developing your lifelong strategy, as these may be things you have never considered important to learn until you identified them as a gap. Identifying the gaps in your knowledge is crucial because it is this that will drive your strategy in the short- and medium-term.

- Blind spots. These are those things you have yet to identify as being necessary for your working life and you will probably be oblivious to them. We do have to be careful about blind spots because we all have them to a greater or lesser extent. Very often they may be pointed out to us by a third party which makes them all the more difficult to deal with. This is where a coach and/or mentor can prove to be very helpful because they will help to identify your blind spots before they cause you and your career damage. Blind spots are often behavioural rather than technical in nature, and will relate to how you are perceived by your peers, subordinates, and superiors (in an organizational, not intellectual sense), and this is the reason why they are often so painful to deal with.

At the end of this assessment you will have:

- captured your current skill and knowledge profile;

- assessed your levels of explicit and implicit knowledge;

SMART VOICES

Eddy Knasel, John Meed and Anna Rossetti, authors of *Learn for Your Life*, describe the concept of the learning lifeline. They believe that in order to grasp both planned and incidental learning opportunities, you need to look critically at your past, present, and future learning. To do this requires an analysis of past learning to understand, amongst others, what factors helped the learning process to succeed, and an assessment of future learning needs based upon your career aspirations and the goals of the organization. Once complete, it is then possible to construct your immediate learning needs that will move you towards your future goals.

- highlighted your knowledge gaps; and

- identified some and, if you are lucky, all of your blind spots.

Future profile assessment

It is now a good idea to develop a future profile which identifies the depth and breadth of skills, attitudes and behaviours you need two to three years from now. When creating this second profile, it will be necessary to revisit your goals to ensure this new profile matches your career objectives. You should recognize that these two stages can be iterative and therefore you should be prepared to pass through them at least twice. I think if you cannot stabilize your profile after three or four iterations then it might be necessary to seek out some professional career advice or seek help from your

SMART PEOPLE
TO HAVE ON
YOUR SIDE:

STEPHEN
STUMPF
AND
JOEL DELUCA

- Authors of *Learning to Use What You Already Know*.
- Offer 33 insights into harnessing your existing knowledge.
- Believe that learning to deal with change is like a surfer learning to ride the waves.
- Assert that being able to respond to change requires the combination of continuous learning and developing new insights.

coach/mentor if you have one. Once you have a defined set of goals and a target knowledge profile, it is useful to compare this with the one produced during the current state assessment. If they look almost identical, then you are either not being honest with yourself, or your skills are precisely what is needed in the future. It may also highlight your lack of knowledge about the world of work and how it might need to change over the coming years. If this is the case, you may find that you have a significant blind spot in the environment category of your knowledge that needs to be addressed. More realistically, you should expect some major differences between the two profiles. Some of the skills may have gone entirely, or moved from low to high (or vice versa); new ones may have appeared. For example, if you aspire to attaining a senior management or board position in your career, then skills such as leadership and motivation are likely to factor.

Skill categorization

The final part of this stage of developing your lifelong strategy should focus on categorizing the types of skills and knowledge you need in the future using the following categorization:[2]

1   Commodity skills. These are skills that are general to any role or any business. They can be picked up very quickly by most people. They include following processes, positive attitudes and behaviours, and low

Admitting that you need to learn something new is always difficult. It is even harder if you are a senior manager who is accustomed to the automatic deference which people accord you owing to your position. But if you don't fight it, that very deference may become a wall that isolates you from learning new things.

Andrew Grove[3]

level skills such as typing, word processing, and so on. Other types of skill also fall into this category, such as technical maintenance and machine minding (such as in a factory). We all need commodity skills, but to maximize our earnings throughout our careers and to gain the most satisfaction, we need to move beyond these. Furthermore, if we look at where the major impact of globalization has been, it has been in the area of commoditized skills, because they are easy to replicate. This explains why so much blue-collar activity has been exported overseas, and why pay for those people with only commodity skills has been falling in the industrialized world.

2   Leveraged skills. These are skills that are not company specific but more complex, and typically more valuable to some companies than others. The best way to think about these skills is how much value you can derive from them externally. Consultancies provide a good model, as they have a wealth of intellectual capital which they can sell on to their clients. The breadth and depth of the skills and expertise available, together with the ability to bring in other cross-sector experiences, is how the consultancies add value. Although many organizations have similar skills internally, they are often unable to concentrate them when required, plus they are not always able to break through the barriers to change. This is why clients are willing to pay such high fees for consultancy support. Similarly, there will be skills within a company that are highly valued and highly rewarded. Understanding which skills these are and whether you have them (or need them) is very useful. As we saw in Chapter 2, testing yourself against the job market and job advertisements is an excellent way to assess which of your skills fall into the leverage category.

3   Proprietary skills. These are the skills and knowledge that are company specific and which a company will pay a premium for because they translate into the wider company brand. Think of Coca-Cola, Disney,

Mercedes-Benz, and similar companies. Each develop and utilize their unique blend of skills to create products and services that command respect and loyalty amongst their customers. In a similar vein, there are skills and knowledge that are valued in the workplace that you possess and which you can command a premium for. It is important, however, to recognize that such skills are company specific, and although this does not mean they are not portable, they do have to be repackaged to suit any new employer. This is principally because each organization has its own way of doing things defined by its culture and, in order to fit in, you will need to make the tacit knowledge explicit so that you can repackage it for your new employer.

This categorization helps you to identify which of your skills:

- Add significant value and are easy to replace.

- Add little value and are easy to replace.

- Add little value and are difficult to replace.

- Add significant value and are difficult to replace.

Smart things
to say about
lifelong learning

If we are not moving forwards,
we are more than likely
falling backwards.

Ideally you should be aiming to have knowledge that has a lot of value and is difficult to replace. The more value-adding skills you have that are in demand, the more secure your future will be. But key to exploiting the knowledge you have is understanding where it is and how to exploit it.

You are now ready to determine your options for moving your strategy forward. As we saw in Chapter 4, there can be no learning without action.

Stage 3 – determine your options

Once you have established your goals and have identified the gaps between your current and future knowledge, the next thing to do is to determine what you need to do to close the gap. But, rather than jump straight to a single course of action, it is better to explore the wider options. This stage is therefore designed to answer the following questions:

- What could you do to shift from where you are now to where you want to be (as defined by your goals)?

- What alternatives are available?

- What approaches have you seen used in similar circumstances?

- Who might be able to help?

- What constraints do you have to work within (time, money etc.)?

- If the constraints were removed, what would you do?

- Which of the options interest you?

When exploring how you will achieve your career and lifelong learning objectives, you should consider the following (these and a number of others are addressed in the next chapter, so time won't be spent discussing them here):

- Changing jobs.

- Moving functions within your current role.

- Training.

- E-learning.

- Action learning.

- Coaching and mentoring.

- Getting involved with projects and other one-off initiatives.

Smart quotes

When people are put into positions slightly above what they would expect, they're apt to excel.

Richard Branson

During this stage it is necessary to take an objective view of the options rather than going for the most obvious or the most attractive. Sometimes it means taking a risk and placing yourself out on a limb. Moving outside of your comfort zone is uncomfortable but it does accelerate learning considerably. To help you review your options objectively, I strongly advise you to use De Bono's six thinking hats (see 'Smart people to have on your side' below). This allows you to review your options across both the emotional and non-emotional dimensions and will help you to assess all the options in an even-handed way rather than allowing yourself to be ruled by either your head or your heart. If you have a coach or mentor, you might want to do this with them.

The other thing you might choose to do is to assess each of the options along the three dimensions of:

- Cost. What will the option cost in terms of money, time, or personal sacrifice?

- Benefit. What will the option provide you with in terms of learning and career development and progression?

- Leading international authority in the field of conceptual thinking.
- Wrote *Six Thinking Hats*. The hats allow us to separate our thinking into six distinct modes, represented by six coloured 'thinking hats'.
- Putting on a hat focuses the thinking, and switching hats redirects it. The six hats and their meanings are:
  - White – facts, figures, and objective information.
  - Red – emotions and feelings.
  - Black – logical and negative thoughts.
  - Yellow – positive and constructive thoughts.
  - Green – creativity and new ideas.
  - Blue – control of the other hats and thinking steps.

SMART PEOPLE
TO HAVE ON
YOUR SIDE:

EDWARD DE
BONO

- Risk. What dangers will the option present in terms of such things as failure?

Ranking each option by reviewing the costs, benefits, and risks of each will help you to decide which of the options you will adopt in your strategy (see Table 6.1).

Table 6.1 An example cost, benefit, risk assessment.

Option	Cost	Benefit	Risk	Rank
Change jobs to seek greater responsibility	Loss of current network and moving outside of comfort zone	Increase in salary and position	May fail, could be made redundant (last in, first out)	2
Move into a new function	Will need to start again to win peoples' trust within the new function	Will widen experience, may improve promotion prospects	May not get on with new colleagues	3
Leave work and undertake some postgraduate training, such as an MBA	Could run into thousands of pounds, will miss out on career opportunities for the next 12–24 months	Will advance learning significantly and could lead to a large increase in salary and lead to better long-term career opportunities	The employment market may change whilst studying, making it difficult to re-enter the employment market	1

Smart quotes

There are two parts of an effective learning strategy … First build a wide repertoire of transferable skills, that is, skills that are not likely to become obsolete anytime soon, and will make you more valuable no matter where you go or what you do … Second, be a knowledge worker no matter what you do. That means you need to leverage skill, knowledge, and wisdom in every project you undertake, every task you accomplish, and every responsibility you assume.

Bruce Tulgan

Stage 4 – what next?

This final stage is about action planning. You will have created the basis of your lifelong learning strategy in the previous three stages, and now it is time to assess how you are going to implement it by deciding on which of the options you looked at in the previous stage you are going to take. This stage is designed to answer the following questions:

- What are the next steps?

- Will these address your goals?

- When will you take them?

- What might get in the way?

- How will you ensure that the next steps are taken?

- Who needs to know?

- How will you get the support you need?

Like any form of planning, it is worth spending enough time on this to ensure that your plan is capable of delivering your strategy. It is best to draw up a short document that summarizes your strategy (see Fig. 6.3 for an example). This should cover:

- Your career goals over the next two to three years.

- Your lifelong learning goals over the same period.

- Your strategy for achieving each of these (for example, change job, take a degree, and so on).

- What specific actions you will take.

Career and learning strategy 200x to 200y

Career goals
- To set up and run a consultancy business, specialising in strategy and project management.

- To be employing 20 consultancy staff and be known in the industry as a thought leader.

Lifelong learning goals
- To gain an understanding of running a business, including marketing, sales, and administration.

- To gain an understanding and practical experience of employment practices and HR.

- To develop strong project management and strategy formulation skills.

Strategy
- Over the next two years, I will change jobs in order to gain business and operational management experience.

- Within the next 36 months, I will become involved with projects and during this time I will seek professional qualifications in project management.

- I will publish five articles on project management and strategy over the next 18 months.

- I will speak at conferences and seminars on topical issues on strategy and project management.

Success criteria

- Company turnover increasing year on year.

- Company is well known with a strong brand and reputation.

- Increasing client base.

- Well known conference speaker.

Fig. 6.3   A basic action plan.

- When you will take these actions (which could be monthly actions, six-monthly, or perhaps annually).

- How you will know you have achieved what you set out to achieve. Such measures of success are vital as they prevent you from deluding yourself that you have succeeded when you haven't, and stop you from making excuses.

This should cover a maximum of two pages and should be kept in your briefcase. Then, every month of so, pick it up, re-read it and assess your progress. Naturally there will be times when progress is slow, but the very act of committing the strategy to paper and reviewing it will ensure you generally keep on track. The other thing to remember is that you may have to revise your strategy as you achieve your objectives and as things change in the world around you. This is a living document which will change as you change; lifelong learning is not a one-off exercise, it is a commitment to continuously develop, learn, and grow. If you have a coach or mentor, it would be an excellent idea to share your strategy with them so that they can help you monitor your progress. There is nothing better than having someone else reminding you of what you have set out to do, as it is well known that people find it much harder to give up something when they have made a public commitment to doing it. In the next chapter we explore some of the options which will help you to implement your strategy.

Notes

1   See Stumpf, S. & DeLuca, J. (1994) *Learning to Use What You Already Know*. San Francisco: Barrett-Koehler Publishers, pp. 107–115.

2   Stewart, T. (1997) *Intellectual Capital: The New Wealth of Nations.* New York: Currency-Doubleday, p. 89.

3   Grove, A. (1997) *Only the Paranoid Survive: How to Exploit the Crisis Points that Challenge Every Company and Career.* London: Harper-Collins Business, p. 145.

7

Implementing Your Strategy

Implementing your lifelong strategy requires you to use as many of the channels and resources that are available to you as possible. Keeping an open mind during the learning process is essential, and on this basis you should never underestimate the wealth of learning opportunities before you. These range from the more mainstream, such as traditional training courses, to the more offbeat, such as using actors and writing a book. The more channels you use, the richer your learning will be and the easier it will be for you to implement your strategy. The other key

Smart quotes

There's a simple psychological principle that says if we do things differently, it helps us think differently, and alternative thinking easily leads to innovative action.

Dr Know

thing about implementing your strategy is that you should never give up, as the world is littered with those who have tried, but failed. Persistence is everything, as we saw with the great inventors, scientists, and entrepreneurs in Chapter 5. As you implement your strategy, you will also begin to experience the draw of the paradox of learning, described in Chapter 4. This will help to stimulate the intrinsic motivation of lifelong learning.

Smart things to say about lifelong learning

Don't try to do it, do it. Trying provides you with all the excuses you need to give up. How about dropping 'trying' from your vocabulary?

Traditional training and education

Despite the advent of the Internet and the opportunities it presents for learning, the traditional forms of learning are still very relevant. For example, just under 84 per cent of training managers use face-to-face courses in preference to the Internet.

Smart quotes

The ratio of smash hits scored to number of shots taken rarely alters with age, so there's no magical life-stage after which we might as well give up striving.

Dr Know

Traditional classroom-based training takes on a variety of forms and is not just restricted to those provided through your workplace. So, consider things like adult education, distance learning and, if it is available, your company's corporate university (see Chapter 1).

To get the full benefit out of any form of training, however, requires that the trainee has the motivation to learn. Without this, nothing will be learnt and nothing will change. The same applies to you and how you use training courses. If you are not sufficiently motivated, you will have wasted your time, and maybe spoilt the course for others. Having been a trainer in the past, there is nothing worse than someone who can't be bothered to learn. These people are not worth having in your organization and they are certainly not worth wasting your valuable training budget on. Always remember that there are many different approaches to learning, not just those you are familiar with.

Smart things to say about lifelong learning

A man who is going nowhere will always be sure that that is exactly where he will arrive.

Verdi wrote operas spanning a period of 50 years because he was determined to develop his skills and expose himself to new ideas.

E-learning

The Internet provides a huge resource for those who pursue lifelong learning. No longer restricted to libraries and books, the Internet allows individuals to share knowledge and learn from others more rapidly than ever before. With millions of sites dedicated to single subjects, chat rooms where it is possible to swap ideas and offer advice, and online universities and learning resources providing distance learning via the Web, learning has never been easier for the individual. Moreover, the Internet provides a rich environment that can bring the learning process alive with a mix of graphics, self-assessments, video, audio, and real-time interaction. As technology advances, especially that associated with networking, the value of e-learning will increase significantly. There are already many e-learning providers that can facilitate your on-line learning. The beauty of these is that they provide a ready-made environment for learning and can save you enormous amounts of time searching for the relevant material yourself. Here are two:

- Learning Matters (www.learningmatters.com). Learning Matters is a virtual learning centre that contains in excess of 1500 resources for the corporate and personal learner. The site offers a wealth of learning solutions, including: training videos from Video Arts, self-development resources published by Echelon Learning, management articles and case studies from MCB University Press and Thomson Learning, e-based diag-

SMART PEOPLE TO HAVE ON YOUR SIDE:

GUISEPPE VERDI

Smart things to say about lifelong learning

Training people who lack the motivation to learn is like soaking raisins to produce grapes ... all you end up with is fat, juicy raisins.[1]

nostic and audit solutions from Echelon Learning, and an international encyclopaedia and management books from Thomson Learning. The site is well organized, up to date, and, for the self-directed learner, reasonably priced. The Virtual Learning Centre offers just-in-time training suitable for a wide range of learning styles. The resource can be accessed via the Web, or can be hosted on an organization's Intranet.

- NoonTime University (www.noontimeu.com). NoonTime University offers educational courses for busy professionals who can't get away from work. This innovative site offers some 40 three-hour, high-impact, tailored courses covering management, administration, and more general subjects over lunch periods and early evening. This addresses the common complaint that it can be very difficult to fit in longer training courses in a busy work schedule.

Books and journals

Books and journals are a ready source of information and knowledge. Both provide you with the opportunity to tap into other peoples' ideas, best practices, and experiences without the need to carry out the research or make the same mistakes or, indeed, have the same insights as the authors did. When you need immediate and up-to-date research, journals are the best source of information. When this is not the case, books are probably the best thing to tap into. Ultimately, a combination of a good library and subscriptions to the more forward-thinking journals, such as the Harvard Business Review, make an ideal combination for continuous learning. There are some real advantages for reading and having an extensive library, including:

- It develops your ability to connect ideas and concepts together in new ways, which itself is one of the major ways in which new ideas are generated.

SMART VOICES

THE UNITED STATES ARMY

On 21st June 2001, the United States Army fully implemented its $600 million Army University Access Online (AUAO) initiative. This will allow enlisted soldiers the opportunity to study for degrees and certificates anytime, anywhere. The AUAO allows its soldiers access to universities, accredited colleges, and technical schools at no cost, through the world's largest online educational portal – eArmyU.com. The AUAO provides access to over 100 certificate and degree programmes, and this will increase as more are added. Soldiers can earn their qualifications from multiple providers using credit transfers across each, thereby allowing army personnel the chance to complete their degrees as quickly and conveniently as possible.

The AUAO includes what the United States Army consider the best-in-class providers of online education programmes, educational services, technology components and services, and project management. Every soldier that enrols onto the programme is provided with a technology package that includes a laptop, printer, Internet Service Provider account, email account and live technology support. In addition, four levels of tutor support are available:

- AUAO level – which provides basic enrolment support to ensure that personnel understand the commitment required to complete their course of study and matching courses to individual learning needs.
- Degree level – once enrolled on a degree or certificate programme, mentors monitor and track an individual's progress through the degree or certificate, and manage issues associated with the institutions involved.
- Course level – online tutors are available to all students.
- Subject level – course level support is augmented by 24 × 7 tutoring services from Smarthinking.com for core courses such as economics and mathematics, as well as an online writing lab and research tools.

- It provides a major source of knowledge and information which you can tap into. So, in the case of the library, you should have books which you will only dip into to support your work as well as those which you will read from cover to cover.

- It allows you to solve business and work problems more readily, without the need to reinvent the wheel.

- It sets you aside from your colleagues and can result in you becoming an unofficial chief knowledge officer.

Smart quotes

The reading of good books is like a conversation with the best men of past centuries; in fact like a prepared conversation in which they reveal only the best of their thoughts.

Descartes

One of the most interesting insights I had when I first started writing was that so few people read the books they bought. When I mentioned to my publisher that I read extensively, her reply was, 'do you read the complete book?' When I replied that I did, she was surprised, as most people tend to give up before they reach the end. The thing that struck me about this was that failing to complete the book meant that the significant nugget that would have made the book worthwhile would, more likely than not, have been missed. We can conclude that those people who read books from cover to cover and also extensively will have a very significant advantage over their colleagues. The bottom line is that books and journals provide knowledge in a pre-packaged form that, if taken seriously, can enhance your learning manyfold. Why develop something from scratch when you can fast track the outcome by building on what is already known?

Coaching and mentoring

Coaching is increasingly an attractive proposition for busy executives, and many organizations now take the trouble to provide mentoring and coaching for their staff, especially those who show potential. It is important to know the difference between coaching and mentoring. Whereas the former is much more active with the coach working through issues with the executive, the latter is more like a sounding board. Second, coaches do not usually have a deep technical knowledge of what you do, they are there to coach, not teach. Their role is to bring out the best from you and to explore ideas with you without the critical eye of the technical expert. Dennis Kinlaw, author of *Coaching for Commitment*,[2] believes that coaching takes on four forms, and it is the combination of these that results in an effective outcome for the coachee. The four forms are:

Smart quotes

The record shows that no one is over the hill till they decide to reduce their time and commitment to their endeavours. The only necessity is that they never stop learning.

Dr Know

1   Generic coaching, which seeks to provide a general understanding about problems that need resolution and develop a degree of self-sufficiency within the coachee, especially when it comes to taking action.

2   Mentoring, which attempts to develop a better understanding of the organization in which you work, although this can be more widely focused (see below).

3   Tutoring, which is aimed at increasing someone's competence in a particular discipline, or at widening the tutee's breadth of knowledge. In both cases, it is designed to increase the capacity and commitment to learning.

4   Confronting, which deals with the shortfalls in our capabilities and performance.

Mentors are generally knowledgeable about your role/profession and can give more technical feedback and support. The most effective form of mentoring is that which takes place outside of the line (or work) relationship, because it ensures objectivity and limits the potential conflicts of interest that could arise. Good mentors are able to suspend judgement, build rapport, co-develop development objectives, and provide feedback. There are four types of coach:[3]

- The directive and challenging coach who directs the learner throughout the learning process.

- The directive and nurturing guardian who acts as a role model and provider of advice.

- The nurturing and non-directive counsellor who provides support during the learning process.

- The challenging and non-directive network/facilitator who helps the individual take charge of their own learning.

Smart quotes

Coaching works for many reasons that overlap and intertwine, but one of the strongest threads in this weave is action. In fact, it's the cycle of action and learning, over time, that leads to more action based change.

Laura Whitworth, Henry Kimsey-House and Phil Sandahl

Although organizations provide mentoring for their staff, this is typically work focused and does not explore anything that is not work related. The purpose of mentoring within the confines of an organization is to provide some career guidance for those being mentored. Unfortunately, the individual being mentored is always half concerned with confidentiality and is often unwilling to share all of their concerns with their mentor. The advantages of external coaches and mentors is that they can be truly objective and the person being coached has the opportunity to really open up. The value that can be derived from an effective coaching relationship should not be underestimated and is a powerful way to enhance your performance and test out new ideas. Moreover, coaches can provide a rapid form of feedback that is often lacking in today's workplace.

Feedback

Learning, as we know is all about feedback. Without the feedback loop we would be unaware of what works and what doesn't and we would fail to develop in every sense of the word. Feedback involves four very simple steps:

- Step 1 – plan to do something.

- Step 2 – do it.

- Step 3 – check the outcome.

- Step 4 – take some action in light of the feedback.

This process is known as single loop learning and is fine for our personal lives when we have the immediacy of feedback. However, within the working context, it is rare to receive such immediate feedback because organizations are very complex and it can take time for the feedback from a decision

THOMAS HOLMES

My son Thomas was recently taking part in his school's charity week. This involves pupils designing and running stalls to attract their fellow pupils and convince them to part with their money. Thomas had dreamt up a historical quiz based around military history. Prizes consisted of small cars and a big bar of chocolate for anyone who got all 12 questions correct. On the day, things did not go according to plan; in fact, no one visited Thomas' stall because the game was too hard. Rather than hang around, Thomas acted on the feedback and changed tack. He sold all of his cars at 40 pence each and the bar of chocolate for £2.50 (it only cost 99 pence). The result? Within half an hour he had sold everything and made £16 – the most in his entire school. This is why acting on feedback works.

SMART VOICES

or action to come through. So, to combat this, we have to deliberately seek out feedback from those around us. This is known as double loop learning and typically involves using the feedback to adjust our mental models and, where appropriate, using external processes, benchmarks, and other data to assess the validity of the decision or action.

A useful technique to use when soliciting feedback from someone is the Johari Window (see Fig. 7.1). This helps to uncover those things that remain unsaid or hidden from another person. The beauty of the Johari Window is that it widens our understanding of ourselves and how the people around us perceive us. It can also be very helpful when working in teams, as to be truly effective, there must be a lot of mutual understanding.

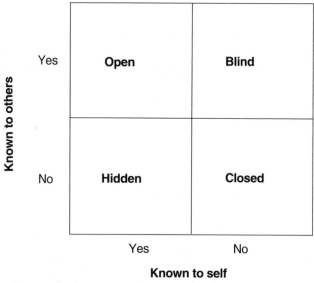

Fig. 7.1   The Johari Window.

The four quadrants are:

- Open. This is where most of us communicate. This is where those around you know what you know, in essence what you are willing to share about yourself, your feelings, view points, and knowledge.

- Blind. Here, others know things about you that you are ignorant of and so they remain hidden from you. Such things tend to be behavioural in nature, but because of the nature of relationships, people are often unwilling to tell you about them. Unfortunately, these can be major inhibitors to learning and especially progression within the workplace.

- Hidden. This is the classic hidden agenda where you know something but will not pass it onto a third party. This may be what you want to achieve, or knowledge you have about an important topic, and so on.

- Closed. These are things that neither you nor those around you know about you. This is the tacit knowledge and understanding that was discussed in Chapter 3.

The Johari Window can be an effective way to gain a more comprehensive understanding of yourself and your knowledge. As you implement your strategy, you should aim to reduce your personal blind spots as much as possible. Ultimately, what you choose to remain hidden is your choice and no one else's, but just remember that if this is knowledge or something that can benefit you, such as improving your personal brand, for example, it might be worth shifting it into the open quadrant.

Use of actors

Increasingly, actors are moving outside of their traditional working environment of the theatre and into the world of the corporates. This is unsurprising given the interest that many organizations have in developing the types of skills and capabilities found within actors. Actors are trained to switch into particular roles, they can turn on their emotions at a drop of a hat, and they are comfortable with audiences. In addition, they possess presence and can use space to create impact and excitement. Organizations are turning to actors to train their staff and develop their interpersonal and presentation skills. The great thing about actors is that they can be superb coaches for those who fear making presentations or indeed, any form of public speaking or interaction which they find difficult. They can also help develop verbal and non-verbal skills which are so often lacking in organizations. They are particularly useful during training, where they can take on particular personas within role-playing exercises. Here, they can provide such realism that it is difficult to distinguish between what is real and what is acting. In this sense, they provide a safe environment in which to test out skills such as selling, managing difficult people, and so on. The key thing is that they create such a realistic environment that it is impossible to separate the training session from reality. A number of commercially orientated acting groups have emerged over the past few years who service both businesses and individuals, and many of these have developed long-term relationships with large corporates. I believe that actors can be a valuable part of any lifelong learning strategy, either as part of an organization's development process, or for the individual who is seeking coaching on a specific concern.

Projects

Getting involved with projects of any kind is one of the best ways to learn new skills and develop capabilities that are both valuable to you and your

KELLOGG GRADUATE SCHOOL OF MANAGEMENT[4]

The Kellogg Graduate School of Management at Northwestern University
has introduced drama into its advanced management programmes. Actors
and theatre directors are used to coach business executives in the use of
drama to allow them to get the most out of their co-workers, subordinates,
and clients. The coaching involves the use of intensive role-playing exercises
designed to test and stretch the business executives and make them more
aware of how their behaviour impacts others.

SMART VOICES

employer. When thinking about getting involved with projects, it is a good
idea to consider what you want to get out of them. It may be to acquire a new
skill, or to increase your knowledge about your organization. Whatever the
reason, projects offer an environment that can accelerate learning because
they usually involve out-of-the-box thinking, the application of planning and
strategic management skills, and a large dose of team working. And, once
you have been involved with a few projects, it is unlikely that you would
want to spend time performing repetitive operational duties. Fortunately,
the importance of projects is increasing as change becomes the norm.

Job and career changes

The one thing that you must get used to is the necessity of job changes and
even changes in careers. The nature of working life is such that none us of

Smart quotes

The world of project managers is very different. Because we are faced
with a unique problem of opportunity, the 'rules' for how the project
should be configured and run have not been developed. In effect, we have
to learn some lessons as we progress.

Jeffrey Pinto and O.P Kharbanda

can afford to become stagnant and one of the best ways to make progress in your career is to change jobs. If you are ambitious, a useful rule of thumb to apply is that if you are not progressing within a two to three year period it is best to move to another employer. Although there are many difficulties associated with changing jobs, such as having to get to know a new organization, its culture, and people, there are major benefits to be had. These include the opportunity to take on more important roles, the chance to increase your seniority, and the ability to get involved with more challenging activities. It normally takes somewhere between eight months and a year before you begin to feel comfortable in the new job and by two years you should be more than competent.

Changing jobs every two to three years actually reduces the time to become familiar with the routine of getting used to a new organization. In addition, it develops the coping skills that you need when dealing with any change. Thus, the skills you develop through changing jobs can be translated into the more general arena of change management.

Moving functions or roles within your current job

Some organizations have adopted a strategy of lateral movement as a way of developing their best talent. They recognize that it is better to keep staff engaged and committed to the organization than losing them to the competition. This involves moving employees from one function or business to another every couple of years to ensure they are continuously stretched and developed. There are numerous benefits to be had, including:

- Increased internal communication.

- Productivity improvements through developing a deeper understanding of an organization's functions and businesses.

SMART VOICES

ABB

ABB recognizes that global leaders have to be developed, and of their 25,000 leaders, approximately 500 are destined at any one time to be global leaders. This group are nurtured at an early stage and transferred to other countries to gain the necessary cultural experience and learning to make them successful. Of course, ABB's success is not just down to leadership. The workers themselves also benefit through continuous training which has been increased by a factor of four in recent years. This learning is based around the action learning concept and is often global, with staff from one country being educated in another.

- Greater vision and creativity because it prevents staff from developing tunnel vision and narrow perspectives based upon a single business or function.

- Increased future employability for those that move on because they develop multiple skill sets.

- Enhanced learning because it generates the skill of learning, and most importantly, it gives the people that move confidence in their ability to learn.

This process is similar to changing jobs every couple of years, but is probably less stressful because it is done within a single company. The two year time horizon is key because it avoids the plateau trap, where after two years most people master the skills required to perform their role at an expert level. The period up to the two year mark is characterized by a three month period of inexperience followed by 18 months of rapid learning.[5]

Writing a book

Writing a book on a business topic is a valuable way to implement your lifelong learning strategy; it is said that most people have at least one book in them. Like everything else in life, many people may start to write a book and fail to finish it. So, those who do have an immediate advantage. Although putting pen to paper may seem an odd thing to do when it comes to implementing your strategy, it can add real value.

- Firstly, writing a book requires research. And the process of research forces you to learn more about the subject you are writing about and therefore increases your personal knowledge and intellectual capital. It also opens up your lateral thinking skills as you draw the material for the book together and develop new insights.

- Secondly, it increases your profile both within your own organization and, more importantly, within the wider marketplace, both of which are essential to your longevity in the world of work. Internally, it sets you aside from those around you and helps to develop your personal brand. But, more importantly, it raises your profile beyond your current employer which can pay dividends later on.

Smart quotes

In your career, knowledge is like milk. It has a shelf-life stamped right on the carton. The shelf-life of a degree in engineering is about three years. If you're not replacing everything you know by then, your career is going to turn sour fast.

Louis Ross

- Thirdly, it allows you to reflect the material you have written about onto your daily work. This can be extremely valuable because it leads to new insights and ideas that can be exploited with your current employer, or your clients.

If you choose to follow this path, make sure your idea is attractive, do your research, and never write the book speculatively: get a contract and then write. At least you can guarantee it will be printed (well, pretty much anyway).

Networking

None of us are islands. As the nature of work has changed, there has been an increased tendency to network beyond our current workplace. More and more people deliberately seek out new contacts that can be added to their network of professionals who can add value to their careers and knowledge. I believe that networking is an effective way to enhance your knowledge and increase your learning. Networking opportunities exist everywhere, but we have to take care to recognize what we want from our networking activities. It might be knowledge, or access to another knowledge network, or it could be opportunity and career development. Whatever the reason, networking is an essential skill for the lifelong learner. One of the most important things to remember about networking is that it cannot be a one-way street. Using your network for personal gain without reciprocal obligation will eventually shut it down. It is necessary to give as much as you get and to give away your knowledge. In this way, people will see you as someone who can help them, thereby establishing a reciprocal relationship.

> **Smart quotes**
>
> Networking is the process of gathering, collecting and distributing information for mutual benefit of you and the people in your network.
>
> Donna Fisher and Sandy Vilas

Communities of practice

During our working lives we tend to work in groups, either defined by the functional role we are undertaking, the profession we have chosen to follow, or the type of projects we get involved in. These groups provide an environment in which we can learn and understand about our jobs, the working environment, and the organization in general. Such learning is unstructured in so far as it is passed from person to person by word of mouth, demonstration, and support. Those with whom we work are a significant source of information, which, during the early stages of our career, are criti-

SMART PEOPLE
TO HAVE ON
YOUR SIDE:

DONNA FISHER
AND
SANDY VILAS

- Donna Fisher is the founder and president of discovery seminars of Houston and a national authority on the importance of people skills and networking ; Sandy Vilas is the president of Coach University, the world's largest training organization for personal and business coaches.
- Authors of *Power Networking: 55 Secrets for Personal and Professional Success.*
- Believe that every networker should follow the ten commandments of networking:
  1 Give up the 'Lone Ranger' mentality.
  2 Honour your relationships.
  3 Acknowledge people.
  4 Manage yourself as a resource.
  5 Take the initiative.
  6 Be your own best PR person.
  7 Ask for what you want.
  8 Expand your horizons.
  9 Follow the golden rule of networking.
  10 Network as a way of life.

cal. These groups are also known as communities of practice. The concept of a community of practice was introduced by Etienne Wegner in her book, *Communities of Practice: Learning, Meaning and Identity.* Communities of practice are a key component in the workplace and are relevant to lifelong learning. A community of practice is defined by three components:

- Mutual engagement and relationships. The nature of work dictates that the majority of people are engaged in similar tasks or require mutual engagement from others to complete them. For example, the claims processing department within an insurance company can be considered to be a community of practice because everyone is involved with the end-to-end process of managing the claims process. Successful communities of practice depend on well-developed interpersonal relationships that are sustained over a long period of time. Without this it can be difficult to establish consistent outcomes and develop the feedback loops required to foster learning.

- Joint enterprise. Mutual engagement requires a joint enterprise that brings people together. As such it depends on the ability of people to negotiate roles and assume responsibilities and accountabilities for getting the job done as part of a well-oiled machine. Communities of practice are part of a wider network of practices that form the corporation. As such they will have their own identity and history and work under constraints imposed by the wider enterprise such as finance, technology, and people.

- Shared repertoire. The third component is the development of a shared repertoire that is about how work gets done. This includes processes, jargon, routines, tools, stories, symbols, and actions taken on a daily basis. In many respects it creates a micro-culture within the corporation and in essence is 'the way we do things round here'.

Anyone new to a community of practice knows that it takes time to understand how things are done, where people sit within the hierarchy, how processes work, and so on. In short, it requires them to learn. Through mutual engagement, the community as a whole continuously learns as it adjusts to incremental and stepwise change within their own and the wider network of communities in which they exist. If you think carefully about your current role and those people you mix with, it should be clear that you spend the majority of time with people who are quite similar to yourself. The adage, 'birds of a feather flock together', is applicable here. So, when it comes to developing new skills it is important to tap into those communities of practice that can help you to learn. If your networking works, it should serve to accelerate your learning, especially when you move from one community of practice to another.

Implementing your lifelong learning strategy can be hard work, but it can also be a lot of fun. And, as you get used to learning, you will find yourself actively seeking out every opportunity that allows you to grow. Ironically, this will make the achievement of your career and learning goals a whole lot easier, as your employer will see you as someone who is willing to adapt and change. The channels you use to enhance your knowledge and capabilities are very much a personal choice, but if I were to rank them into some kind of order, this is where I would place them (and why). Naturally, they are all important means for implementing your lifelong learning strategy and none of them should be underestimated.

1 Job and career changes. Although the hardest, it is a great way to accelerate learning, especially during the first nine months of a new job.

2 Moving functions. If you don't change jobs that much, change functions. This will also get you used to learning and applying new skills.

3 Projects. These are unique undertakings which require a mix of skills and an ability to work outside of your comfort zone. There can be no gain without pain.

4 Coaching and mentoring. If you get the right coach or mentor, they can be of immense value. Why? Because they will constantly hold a mirror up to yourself and help you identify and address some of the many blind spots you have. They also offer guidance and challenge you as you progress through your working life.

5 Feedback. Whenever this is given in an objective manner it is valuable. And remember, don't always ask your superiors; your peers and subordinates have valid views about you too. Seek them out.

6 Communities of practice. If your are new to a job, then tapping into the knowledge (both explicit and tacit) within the community of practice in which you find yourself, is a useful way to accelerate your understanding of your new role and to learn some of the tacit rules that go with any job.

7 Books and journals (including writing a book). These are greatly underestimated and, because so few people really use books as a learning tool, I have dropped them down in the rankings. I personally feel that books are one of the best sources of accelerated learning around, and a great way to plug the gaps in your knowledge.

8 Networking. This is less of a learning tool and more of a way of accessing other peoples' knowledge and experience.

9 Training (traditional and e-learning). Training, in whatever form is useful and as long as you are able to put into practice what you have learnt, can be effective. For many of us though, training is rather like learning to pass your driving test; the real learning takes place after the test and many perceive training to be too similar to their school days and don't really want to do it anyway.

10 Use of actors. Actors are great for improving your intrapersonal and interpersonal skills, especially when dealing with social occasions.

Learning from the unexpected

So far we have dealt with the deliberate steps you can take whilst implementing your lifelong learning strategy. But this in itself is not enough as

Smart quotes

It is always interesting to see how much society learns from a crisis. Consider the effects of Bhopal on the chemical and safety industries, the Challenger on the aerospace industry, AIDS on the insurance and medical research industries, or the Gulf War on the global military situation. Each of these events was not expected. Each occurred because no one with sufficient authority to change the course of events was thinking such things would happen. Whether or not these events could have been prevented (i.e. controlled) is irrelevant to what can be learned now they did happen.

Stephen A. Stumpf and Joel R. DeLuca

there is, of course, one piece missing, and that has to do with your ability to embrace the unexpected events that occur and view these as learning opportunities. Departures from the expected ensure that we avoid becoming complacent with our surroundings or about what we know.

The real beauty of the unexpected is that it forces us to sit up and take note. Such events are usually too much of a shock to ignore and require a positive response. The key thing is to take these opportunities to learn and develop new perspectives on what we do. The danger of not learning is that we become destined to repeat the same mistakes the next time such events occur.

Smart quotes

Clever people learn from others' mistakes. Fools learn from their own.

Alexander Lebed

Learning from success and failure

It is essential that we learn from our mistakes and, more importantly, we must be able to learn from other peoples'. Equally critical is the ability to learn from your and other

SMART VOICES

NIKE RESPONDING TO THE RISKS OF GLOBALIZATION[6]

Back in 1994, the annual salary of Nike's Chief Executive Officer, Phil Knight, was $1.5 million, which was infinitely more than its workers in China received. At that time it would have taken 15 centuries for them to earn the same. This disparity came to a head when a number of non-governmental organizations demonstrated during the opening of Nike's shop in San Francisco. The issue concerned the amounts paid to front line workers (approximately $1.44 per pair) when compared to how much the shoes were actually sold for (approximately $80 per pair). But it also went far beyond just wages and the marking up of products. Issues such as Nike repeatedly shifting production to regions with the cheapest labour costs added to the growing belief that Nike was a poor corporate citizen. At the time, Nike responded by stating that the workers should believe themselves to be fortunate enough to have a job, and that the issues of how much people were paid should be put before the United Nations, rather than Nike. In 1998, Phil Knight responded to the criticisms more positively, initially acknowledging the underestimating of public concern over the issue of worker exploitation. This was followed by a series of new policies designed to improve working conditions through the elimination of hazardous chemicals in the production process, researching into international manufacturing processes, and starting a programme that independently checked the working conditions of the manufacturing plants.

peoples' success. It is rare for people to reflect on either success or failure, and yet there are always insights to be had and lessons to be learnt. There are a number of ways we can learn from success and failure. For example, the UK's National Audit Office publishes reports on failed projects, NLP provides the basis for modelling other people's success, and the use of After Action Reviews (see smart voices) allow us to reflect on recent actions and decisions.

SMART VOICES

THE UNITED STATES ARMY AFTER ACTION REVIEW (AAR)[7]

The United States Army use the AAR as a means of continuous learning and improvement. The AAR originated during the Vietnam War, where the soldiers in the field knew more than those at headquarters. The AAR allows people to learn immediately after an event, irrespective of whether it was a success or a failure. The key thing is that it takes place immediately. Conducting an AAR usually takes between 20 and 30 minutes and should answer the following questions:

- What should have happened?
- What actually happened?
- What were the differences between what should have, and what actually happened?
- What lessons can be drawn from the experience and how can any strengths revealed be built upon, and any weaknesses reduced or eliminated?

Notes

1   Stumpf, S. & DeLuca, J. (1994) *Learning to Use What You Already Know*. San Francisco: Barrett-Koehler Publishers, p. 133.

2   Kinlaw, D. (1993) *Coaching for Commitment: Managerial Strategies for Obtaining Superior Performance*. San Diego: Pfeiffer & Company, pp. 22–2.

3   Clutterbuck, D. (1998) *Learning Alliances*. London: Institute of Personnel and Development, quoted in Hale, R. (1999) 'The dynamics of mentoring relationships: towards an understanding of how mentoring supports learning'. *Continuing Professional Development*, Issue 3.

4 Rifkin J. (2000) *The Age of Access: How the Shift from Ownership to Access is Transforming Modern Life*. London: Penguin Books, p. 166.

5 The Plateau trap was first identified by Judith Bardwick in her book, *The Plateauing Trap*. New York: Amacom.

6 This case study is based upon a discussion on Nike and its approach to corporate affairs and sociability in Schwartz, P & Gibb, B. (1999) *When Good Companies Do Bad Things: Responsibility and Risk in an Age of Globalization*. New York: John Wiley & Sons, pp. 51–55.

7 Collison C. & Parcell, G. (2001) *Learning to Fly: Practical Lessons from One of the World's Leading Knowledge Companies.* Oxford: Capstone, pp. 76–85.

8
Success

We are told that no one but ourselves is responsible for our careers and future. These words have never been truer than they are today. Uncertainty is making it difficult for organizations to offer jobs for life, technology is leading to unprecedented change, and globalization is leading to greater competition and an increasing likelihood that our jobs will be moved overseas. Against this backdrop, the need to ensure that we are as well prepared for the future as possible is increasingly important. But this depends on our ability to learn, not just occasionally and when we have to (which is usually too late), but continuously.

The purpose of this book has been to present a convincing argument for embracing lifelong learning as a strategy for survival, as well as outlining the areas that you should attend to, and how to develop and implement

> *Smart quotes*
>
> Bodies can suffer from unrelieved repetition and so can minds and lives. Rather than a Friday drink, try drama classes. Rather than TV, switch over to dancing. The chances are you'll gravitate naturally to some of your new approaches, and find a pleasing balance between the familiar and refreshing.
>
> Dr Know

Smart quotes

It is not the critic who counts, nor the man who points out how the strong man stumbled or where the doer of deeds could have done better. The credit belongs to the man who is actually in the arena; whose face is marred by dust and sweat and blood; who strives valiantly; who errs and comes up short again and again; who knows the great enthusiasms, the great devotions, and spends himself in a worthy cause; who at the best knows in the end triumph of high achievement; and who at worst, if he fails while daring greatly; so that his place shall never be with those cold and timid souls who know neither defeat or victory.

Theodore Roosevelt

your lifelong learning strategy. Following the advice is not easy, and success will only come through perseverance.

Success in lifelong learning can be boiled down to a small number of key actions. Each of these will help you to assess for yourself the reasons why you need to take concerted action and then put in place the foundations to direct your learning. If you follow these actions, after a period of six months or more, you should be comfortable with the process of lifelong learning, and begin to see some of the rewards.

1   Wise up. The world of work is constantly changing and we must become more aware of what is going on around us. Taking an interest in what is happening on a global as much as a regional scale is essential for anyone who wants to progress in their career. Wising up is therefore all about opening yourself up to what's going on around you and reflecting this upon you, your learning, and your career.

2   Check if you are ready. Making an honest assessment of your current attitudes toward lifelong learning, and of your career to date is the perfect way to place a stake in the ground from which you can move on. This helps you to assess your learning obstacles, determine what you need

to do, and, most importantly, help you to measure how far you have progressed and what benefits you are achieving.

3   Understand how you learn. We all have learning preferences and, in order to learn as effectively as possible, we need to understand our own preferred learning style. This may require a degree of experimentation with the various channels of learning (books, e-learning, coaches, and so on), as you may find one is much more effective than another.

4   Identify your talents, enhance them, and exploit them. Many people pass through life without knowing what makes them special. They waste their talents. If you know what combination of talents makes you special it is a much simpler exercise to build on them and communicate them to other people, especially your employer. After all, if you don't know, how can anyone else? One of the best ways for you to understand what talents you have is to ask your peers and, if you are brave enough and can trust the answer, your boss.

5   Identify your weaknesses. This is a lot harder than it first seems, as it means taking and accepting some honest feedback about what you do and how you do it. Such feedback, as long as it is delivered in the right way, can be highly instructive. Ideally, you should ask for the feedback and, once you have received it, take some time to reflect on it and what it means. Remember the NLP technique of outcome equals event plus response? If you keep your response calm, you will gain more from the process. Understanding what your weaknesses are will allow you to drop those attitudes, behaviours, and skills which are no longer valid or which are holding you back.

6   Develop your lifelong strategy. Despite the rhetoric that suggests strategy is dead, those without one tend to drift. It is far better to have a strategy that sets your career and learning objectives for the next two

to three years than rely on your employer, who will typically serve you a series of platitudes about such things as career deals and then fail to deliver them. Your strategy should seek to balance the intrapersonal, interpersonal, technical, and environmental skills required to succeed in the workplace.

7   Implement your strategy. There is little point in having a strategy without implementing it. Action is required and you should aim to use as many of the learning channels open to you, including reading, traditional training courses, the Internet and e-learning, failure, success, and so on. You should set yourself a series of milestones against which you can measure progress and adjust your strategy accordingly (see action 8, below).

8   Always be prepared to update your strategy. Part of the skill of lifelong learning is knowing when and how to adjust to the changes around you. The very act of learning will make you more sensitized to the wider business and working environments and hence make it easier for you to update your strategy. If necessary, revisit the questions at the start of Chapter 2. It is vital that you check the relevance of your knowledge and skills on a regular basis as this will help you discard that which is no longer useful to you. The most significant benefit of updating your strategy is that it begins to develop the skills of personal change and makes the process of change, whatever its source, an easier thing to cope with.

The future

So what of the future of lifelong learning? It is clear that its importance will grow for everyone. The very survival of individuals, corporations, and in extreme cases, nations will depend on their ability to continuously learn. With an ageing population, the acceleration of technological change, and the competitive forces of globalization, competition for the best talent will hot up. Attracting the best talent will not only mean rewarding them, it will also mean providing them with learning opportunities throughout their career. For those nations and corporations that can provide these opportunities, they will establish a significant competitive advantage over those that don't. As for the individual, it will become increasingly necessary to embrace lifelong learning, especially as knowledge work will become the driving force of the global economy. For those of us that choose to learn continuously, the rewards will be great. Not only will we be able to maintain an unbroken career, we ought to be able to pick and choose the best jobs globally and see our income and standard of living rise.

> Smart things to say about lifelong learning
>
> Atrophy is the only alternative to growth and learning.

Over the next five to ten years, the significance of the Internet as a practical and valuable source of learning will grow. Smart use of content and learning management systems that can adjust to the learning needs and styles of the learner will mean better take-up. The rise of the corporate university will continue and the traditional universities will transform themselves to compete. Organizations will begin to appoint chief learning officers and

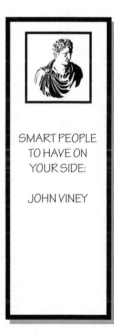

SMART PEOPLE TO HAVE ON YOUR SIDE:

JOHN VINEY

- Chairman, Europe for search firm Heidrick and Struggles.
- Author of the books, *Career Turnaround, One-Man Band, The Culture Wars, Drive-Leaders in Business and Beyond,* and *So You Dream of Being a Chief Executive?*)
- Believes career success can be boiled down into six Cs:
  - courage;
  - certitude;
  - consistency;
  - confidence;
  - clarity; and
  - calm.

Smart quotes

Quite simply, the more we feel in control of fashioning our future, the more we invest in our lives, which in turn increases the likelihood of success.

Dr Know

directors of learning whose sole responsibility will be to ensure the correct processes and mechanisms are in place to allow individuals and organizations to learn.

The future rests with you and your ability to continuously develop. The longer you fail to take action, the harder it will be to begin. So, take some important steps today and start your journey of lifelong learning. The sooner you start, the sooner you will start reaping the benefits. As a parting shot, look at Fig. 8.1 and work out in which quadrant you currently sit and which one you think you ought to. There is no need to explain the model, as it is self-explanatory. Good luck.

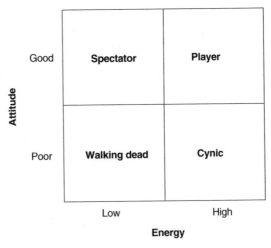

Fig. 8.1 Where do you want to be?

Index